GROWING FOR
BEGINNERS

by

JOHN FALLOWFIELD

AUTHOR'S PREFACE

THE war of 1939—and the years that followed did make people realise, in a way they had never realised before, how much the nation had depended on its fruit supplies from abroad. In consequence more and more garden owners, and even allotment holders, have desired to plant their own fruit trees and bushes so that they can be independent of outside sources. After all, we live in an ideal country for growing fruit and there is no reason at all, why every householder should not have his own supplies.

As in any other craft (and I like to think of gardening as a craft) there are many things to be learned. This book, simply written as it is, is designed to help those who are starting fruit growing and who want to make a success of it. Many ghastly mistakes will be saved if the pages are carefully studied and the advice given followed. As a fruitgrower myself for some thirty years I feel that I can write with some authority.

JOHN FALLOWFIELD.

Contributor to
The Farmers' Weekly, The Estate Magazine,
The Market Grower, etc.

CONTENTS

FRUIT GROWING FOR BEGINNERS

CHAPTER I

TREATING THE SOIL AND FEEDING THE TREES

IT is very fortunate that most fruits will grow on a very wide range of soils and under very differing climatic conditions in Great Britain. The great thing is to keep the tree growing at a steady rate. If it is allowed to grow too fast then there is nothing but leaf and little fruit. If the tree is stunted then the cropping is premature and light in weight. It is, therefore, inadvisable to try and grow fruits, for instance, that dislike a dampish soil on such ground for they will only be stunted as a result. Follow the advice given in the chapters on individual fruits and try and stick to types which will suit your garden rather than try to have a complete range, and have distinct failures in some instances.

Remember that you can't judge soils for fruit trees in the same way you can for vegetables. The roots of fruit trees and bushes may go down 10 ft. or more (gooseberries, for instance, go down 8 ft. even) and so you want to know the sort of soil you have underneath as well as on top. It is well worth while therefore digging out a hole in the garden 3 or 4 ft. deep to see what is down below and to make decisions on what is found there rather than in the top 1 ft. layer. Don't be misled into believing that the richest soil is the best for fruit trees. Rich soils tend to produce too rapid growth.

Give thought to shelter. South Westerly winds are

very common in this country, and it is most annoying to have grown a good crop, and then, have the fruits blown off and damaged, and more annoying still, to find that because of continued winter gales the roots of the trees are loosened in the ground and death is occurring in consequence. Shelter must be given from the East winds too, because these can cause the death of the blossoms, as well as preventing the insects from carrying out their pollination work properly. Even after the petals have fallen, East winds are bad, because they check growth, and many a tiny fruitlet instead of developing properly has shrivelled up under such conditions and dropped to the ground. This incidentally is one of the commonest troubles with black currants, cherries, and gooseberries.

Don't, in providing shelter for your trees, overdo it, or you may produce what is known as a frost-hole, or a frost-trap. The shelter is needed from the two sides from which the prevailing winds normally come, but do not hedge a little fruit plot all round or the cold air will not be able to get away and so fill up the enclosure (like water fills up a depression in the ground) and thus ruin the blossoms. Remember when planting to keep the fruits which like similar feeding together. It is not a bad plan, for instance, with dessert apples to allow grass to grow below them as this in reducing the amount of nitrogen in the soil helps to give better colour.

When testing the soil in the garden it is a good plan to do so in the winter when the soil is wet for bad drainage will make itself evident under such conditions. Sodden soils must be drained or they will only cause the roots of the fruit trees and bushes planted in them to rot. It is usually possible in any garden to bury agricultural drain pipes in such a way as to carry excess moisture away even if it has to go into a well or sump dug for the purpose at the bottom of the garden. The unsuitable soils are those that are shallow, and badly drained.

Before planting the trees or bushes the ground must be dug over well and be cleaned of all perennial weeds. The greatest of care must be taken to give the fruit the right start. Again and again beginners have regretted planting before the land was ready. Don't make the mistake of digging in quantities of dung or rotted vegetable matter. This should be applied as a top dressing afterwards, except in the case of strawberries. The great thing is to see that the land is absolutely clean, even if it means spending hours and hours forking the ground over and picking up the little pieces of couch or convolvulus or any such perennial weeds there may be.

FEEDING THE TREES

Normally, it is said that there are three main plant foods required by trees and bushes, but experiments have tended to show that almost all soils in this country contain sufficient phosphate for the needs of fruit 'trees and bushes. This means that there are only the two other important elements of plant foods, i.e., nitrogen and potash, with which the garden owner has to deal. Different classes of fruits require different proportions of these two. For the purpose of this book it is proposed to classify all fruits into three main classes. 1.—The cooking apples, pears, raspberries, strawberries, loganberries, blackberries, lowberries, etc., these will need heavier applications of nitrogen than class No. 2, although they require regular doses of potash.

2.—Dessert apples, gooseberries and red currants like plenty of potash and show potash starvation symptoms very quickly. They can never use nitrogen unless there is potash present. 3.—Plums, cherries, black currants, nuts, damsons, apricots, peaches and nectarines. These need regular supplies of nitrogen in order that fresh shoot growth can be produced each year on which next year's fruit will be borne. They are nitrogen lovers primarily and they only need potash in moderate quantities.

Before, however, discussing the practical application of the above statements three or four others factors must be borne in mind. First of all, pruning. If you hard prune a tree it seems to have the same effect as giving a heavy dose of nitrogen, for a lot of new growth is produced. If you do not prune a tree at all, or prune it very little, little growth will result. So it can be said that more nitrogen is necessary in the case of a non-pruned tree than in the case of a pruned tree. Secondly, cultivation. If you hoe regularly underneath fruit trees, this has a similar effect to heavy doses of nitrogen. On the other hand if you allow the grass to grow up to the tree much of the nitrogen in the soil will be taken up by the grass and the tree may suffer from nitrogen starvation in consequence. It is seldom necessary to apply potash to trees that are growing in grass. Unfortunately it isn't possible to sow grass under gooseberries and red currants as they are so shallow rooting, and so if they have been given too much nitrogen in the past the answer is to withhold the nitrogen and give potash. Thirdly, root stocks have an effect. Trees are raised by being grafted on to different types of roots and if you have a strong root such as the No. 16 in the case of apples you will not have to give so much nitrogen, for the tree will grow strongly anyway. On the other hand if the apples was on a very dwarfing stock like the No. 9, the tree would be dwarfed and it might be necessary to give some nitrogen. Fourthly, and lastly, if you allow the leaves of your trees to be badly eaten by caterpillars or ruined by aphides they won't be able to carry out their job of manufacturing food and so you may have to give more to the ground in consequence.

Having read these observations, how can the beginner apply the information in a practical manner? It seems that the two foods he must be concerned with are, nitrogen and potash. Nitrogen he can give as sulphate of ammonia, nitrate of soda or nitro-chalk; and the potash he can apply as sulphate of potash or wood ashes. The potash will normally be given in November and the nitrogen in January or February.

APPLES.—Two ounces of sulphate of potash per square yard for the first five years of a tree's life and one ounce per square yard afterward. Broadcast right round as far as the branches spread.

Sulphate of ammonia at two ounces per square yard for cooking apples in January or February, but in the case of dessert apples, only one ounce to the square yard.

For apples growing on grass nitro-chalk at two ounces to the square yard in addition to the above in September.

PEARS.—The same type of manuring as for apples, except that it is only necessary to give potash at one ounce per square yard from the start.

PLUMS.—As the fruits contain a high percentage of moisture and have to grow rapidly during the dry months of the year they should receive mulchings of well-rotted vegetable refuse in the summer (i.e., top dressings) at the rate of one barrow-load to six square yards. This should be forked in lightly in the winter.

In addition, use Cornish Fish Manure at four ounces to the square yard each November, and sulphate of potash at one ounce to the square yard.

CHEERIES.—See Plums.

APRICOTS, PEACHES, NECTARINES.—Treat as for plums but in addition give sulphate of ammonia at two ounces to the square yard early in March.

GOOSEBERRIES.—Every winter give one good barrow-load of well-rotted vegetable refuse to every twelve bushes. In the spring apply half ounce of sulphate of ammonia and two ounces of sulphate of potash per bush.

BLACK CURRANTS.—Give well-rotted vegetable refuse as advised for gooseberries and in November apply sulphate of potash at one ounce per bush. In January give sulphate of ammonia at two ounces per square yard.

RED CURRANTS.—Give two forkfuls of properly composted vegetable refuse to each bush as a top dressing each May. Apply sulphate of potash at the rate of two ounces per bush before planting. Each year give two ounces of sulphate of potash and one ounce of sulphate of ammonia in January.

RASPBERRIES.—Apply properly composted vegetable refuse along the rows each May, as a mulch, at the rate of one good barrow-load per five yard row. Give sulphate of potash at the rate of two ounces each five yard row in November.

BLACKBERRIES, LOGANBERRIES.—See Raspberries.

STRAWBERRIES.—Dig well-rotted vegetable refuse in between the rows, lightly, each winter. Apply Cornish Fish Manure along rows just before blossoming at three ounces per yard run. Give sulphate of potash at two ounces per square yard each November.

CHAPTER II

HOW TO PLAN AND PLANT

NATURALLY the garden owner will be guided by his, or her own likes, or dislikes, when making decisions as to which type of fruits to plant. The man, for instance, who hates blackberries will not put in any. On the other hand, due regard must always be paid to the future and if there are children coming on, then it is always a good plan to have as much fruit about as possible all the year round. Remember that black currants are particularly full of vitamins and are excellent for young children. Red currants on the whole are not so much in demand, for apart from red currant jelly they don't make much of a dish by themselves. They are usually mixed with raspberries or loganberries and servᵉd in a pie or are bottled.

You must consider all members of the household. It is a good thing to have different varieties of apples so as to extend the picking. It is a mistake, for instance, to have an early dessert variety like Worcester Pearmain only, for this will mean that after August there will be no dessert apples to eat at all. In the case of cooking apples it is usually preferable to have keepers than earlies, for a good variety like Edward VIIth will enable a careful house-holder to have good apples to use well after the turn of the year.

In a small garden it is quite convenient to have dual purpose kinds. In the case of an apple, for instance, a variety like Newton Wonder which is an excellent keeper and cooker, and yet is quite a good dessert at Christmas time, or in the case of plums there is Victoria which is excellent as a cooker and as a dessert also. In the case of low-lying gardens that are subject to frost it is advisable to try and plant late flowering varieties which usually escape the frost. In the case of apples there is, for instance, Crawley Beauty. Remember that with strawberries you will have to plant say, one new row each year because the strawberry plant doesn't normally last successfully more than three years, so when planning, think about these extensions and remember that the first row will have to be grubbed up at the end of the third-year period.

Don't waste the walls and fences; see that these are clothed with various fruits, making certain to put the right type on the right walls and fences. For instance, for the North and East walls Morello cherries and gooseberries do best, together with plums like Rivers Early, Czar and Prolific; while on South and West walls, apricots, peaches, nectarines, pears and choice dessert plums do well. West walls and fences do well for cordon apples and pears.

Taking it all round it is much better to plant bush trees on dwarfing stocks rather than planting half-standards which take up such a lot of room. Too often the garden owner does not realise that a standard tree which looks comparatively small when first planted will soon grow and grow and eventually will need a space of at least thirty feet on either side of it. Further, a standard tree usually takes a number of years before it comes into cropping, whereas cordons, or bush trees on dwarfing stocks come into cropping almost immediately. It is always better to go in for a number of dwarf trees than one big tree. You can get greater variety and a longer continuity of supply, for instance, apple trees on the type nine stock might go in as close as ten feet square and that on the triangular plant would give you over 500 trees to the acre. On the other hand if you planted standard apple trees that needed thirty feet square (as they do) you would only get just get over fifty trees to the acre—a tremendous difference.

POLLINATION

Remember when planting that certain fruits are self-sterile. That is to say they need the pollen from another variety flowering at the same time to cause their flowers to set. To put it simply, there are varieties that need a male counterpart before fruit can be expected. The Doyenne du Comice Pear needs the Glou Morceau; the Cox's Orange Pippin needs the James Grieve; the Coe's Golden Drop plum needs Oullin's Golden Gage, and the Early Rivers cherry, its mate Governor Wood. Don't therefore plant self-sterile varieties and expect them to crop without their mates. Either plant self-fertile varieties or plant the self-steriles with their " husbands."

SPRAYING

You won't be able to grow good fruit unless you spray the trees properly. You will learn that in chapter VI. Winter sprays and spring sprays, however, have the habit of damaging crops below. That is why it is a good plan to keep fruit in a patch by itself, rather than try to inter-crop with vegetables. But if you have to intercrop with vegetables then be prepared to cover them up with old sacks while the spraying is going on, so as to ensure that they are not damaged.

Another point in regard to spraying is that some fruits do not like lime-sulphur and yet lime-sulphur is one of the best specifics for controlling fungus diseases on apples and pears and does give good results on gooseberries, against mildew. On the other hand, if yellow goose-berries are being grown, lime-sulphur cannot be used or else the bushes will be completely defoliated. Thus it is a good plan not to plant yellow varieties of gooseberries under apples, lest the lime-sulphur drip should fall upon them. The Davison's Eight black currant is also liable to lime-sulphur damage, as is the Stirling Castle apple.

PLANTING TIMES

It is important to see that the trees and bushes are

planted during the dormant season, but it is always better to get them in, if possible, in October and early November than in January or February. Always plant when the soil is right. It is a mistake to put the roots of trees in the ground when the soil is wet, sticky and lumpy.

It is better to get the strawberries in the ground in July and August and they will give heavier crops over a period of years if planted as early as this.

Planting the tree or Bush. It is always better to dig the holes just before planting. Make the hole big enough so that the roots can be spread out. Don't make it deeper than eight inches or so and never bury the union of stock and scion below ground level. In heavy clay soils it is better to plant on the surface of the ground and to dig earth over the roots.

See that the damaged roots are neatly trimmed by cutting them with a sharp knife on the underside of each root. This causes rapid healing and a growth of new roots. As the soil is being put into the hole, one man should lift the tree up and down gently so that the soil can get in between the roots; after every few spadefuls have been put in a good treading should be done to ensure firmness.

When trees are being planted against a wall, see that the roots are as far from the wall or fence as possible and have the stem sloping slightly towards it.

Staking. It is always worth while seeing that a tree is properly staked, even in the case of bush trees. It is impossible for the tree to make new roots if it is constantly wobbling about and being moved with every wind that blows. Preserve the bottom of the stakes with Cuprinol so that they won't rot away in the ground. Stakes from three or four feet long will usually do for bush trees if they are driven well into the ground at an angle of 45 degrees, pointing in the direction of the prevailing wind. Tie the tree on to the stake by wrapping a piece of sacking six inches wide around the stem of the tree and then using a tie which will ensure that the stake does not rub against the tree. The tie should be taken off each year before tar distillate spraying so that any insects harbouring beneath the band may be removed, and in order to prevent the tie constricting the growth of the tree. Tying should again be done when tar distillate washing is over.

Mulching. Do not allow the trees to suffer from lack of moisture in the spring and summer of the following year, so in the spring or early summer cover the ground for three feet around each tree or bush with well-rotted vegetable refuse, spent hops or lawn mowings to a depth of three or four inches. This will save the tree or bush in a drought.

Protection. Fruit trees hate draughts and if the garden is a small one and there is a path leading down from a back gate, every time the gate is left open a draught of air will blow down. This is one of the commonest causes of failure, for instance, when fruit trees are planted alongside a garden path in such circumstances. Much good can be done under these conditions to prevent a draught by putting up a temporary sacking screen, especially at blossoming time and at fruiting times.

Trees growing against walls can be given protection during blossoming by hanging fish netting in front of the trees. Where birds are a nuisance, black cotton has to be wound in and about the branches or the bushes and canes have to be grown in a cage made of wire netting with a temporary roof of fish netting. The drip from a wire netting roof may do harm to the bushes.

Ripening pears and plums may be protected from birds and wasps if the entire fruits are enclosed in a butter muslin bag or in a transparent paper bag. This should be tied firmly to the branches.

DISTANCES TO PLANT

Apples,	standard	30-40 ft. apart	Pears,	standard	25 ft. apart
„	bush	9-12 ft. „	„	bush	9-12 ft. „
„	cordon	2-3 ft. „	„	cordons	2-3 ft. „
„	espalier	15 ft. „	„	espalier	15 ft. „
Plums,	standard	20 ft. „	Cherries,	standard	30 ft. „
„	bush	15 ft. „	„	bush	
„	fan-trained	12 ft. „		(Morello)	15 ft. „
Damsons, see plums.			„	fan-trained	18 ft. „
Blackberry		12 ft. „	Currants, bush (Red)		5ft. „
			„ „ (Black)		5 ft. „
Gooseberry,	bush	5 ft. „	„ cordon (Red)		1 ft. „
„	cordon	2 ft. „	„ espalier (Red)		5 ft. „
„	espalier	5 ft. „	Loganberry, see Blackberry.		

Strawberries 2ft. 6 ins. between   Rasberries 6 ft. between rows.
   rows.   18 inches in rows.   2 ft. in rows.

CHAPTER III

PRUNING, WHAT IT MEANS AND DOES

THERE are two things to realise first of all when studying pruning. The first is that every tree has got to be pruned in accordance with its individual requirements. There is no rule of thumb method. Secondly, pruning is not an impossible art to learn and any keen amateur may soon master the craft of pruning especially if he will study the cuts he made the previous year and what has happened as a result of them. A beginner can learn more from dealing with his own trees and bushes than from any amount of reading and book study.

There are, however, certain main principles to be followed. The first undoubtedly is, that to cut a growth hard back in the winter, definitely encourages the development of strong new shoots. The harder you cut back (that is to say the more of the young wood you remove) the more growth you'll get. It is better on the whole not to prune at all than to over-prune. However, when you do not prune the tree may quickly become a tangled mass of wood with the result that the fruit will be inferior and it will be more difficult to control pests and diseases.

It must be remembered that the pruning of fruit trees differs according to the age of the tree. For the first five or six years you may prune in order to build up a strong framework of branches on which the fruits of the future will be formed. You may aim to produce a tree whose branches are evenly spaced so that the sunshine and air can get at them easily. You can prune the tree so that it adopts almost any shape you like. It may be cup-shaped; it may have a strong central branch; it may be trained like a pyramid. The pruner can largely decide what shape the tree is to be and so his winter knife work is designed to this end.

Once the tree has been shaped, say after the fifth year, the pruner ceases to cut the growths back as hard as he has done in the past. He starts what is called Light Pruning for he wants to bring the tree into bearing. He is now going to alter his pruning in accordance with the variety that he is tackling. If it is a variety of tree that bears its fruit on short stems (spurs as they are called) close to the main stem, he will cut back the lateral one year old shoots to within three or four buds of their base. If, on the other hand, the fruit concerned is what is called a tip bearer, that is to say it bears on the ends of its lateral growths, naturally it is a mistake to cut these back. This is the case with stone fruits, for instance. With apples and pears it is often a good plan at this stage to cut back the one year old wood in the centre of the tree to within three or four buds of their base and to leave the outside one year old lateral growths long. This induces the trees into fruiting earlier.

Once the trees have started to crop regularly, the winter pruning should be done so as to keep the correct balance. If, for instance, the trees are making nothing but fruit buds, and are tending thus to over-fruit, then the pruning of the end growths or leaders will be severe. It will be necessary to cause a growth; if, on the other hand, there has been a calamitous season, frosts ruined all the blossoms and in consequence the trees made a tremendous amount of wood, then the minimum amount of pruning would be done.

With plums, cherries, and any other stone fruits for that matter, there is very little need to do any shortening of leaders (*i.e.*, end growths) once the trees have come into bearing and so all that need be done when a plum tree is cropping well is just to cut out the growths that tend to be crossing or rubbing, and those which are diseased or damaged. It is important with stone fruits to paint over the cuts thus made in the winter with a thick white lead paint.

SUMMER PRUNING

It is very convenient to do the majority of the pruning in the summer especially after the trees have come into cropping. Summer pruning checks the growth of shoots and roots if done correctly, and induces fruitfulness in consequence. It also ensures that the sun and air gets to the tree and so the wood is well ripened and the fruit beautifully coloured. The simplest way of summer pruning and this applies principally to apples and pears, is to cut back all the side growths that are over 9 inches long to within one or two buds of their base. This work should start in June and should continue throughout July, August and early September. In every case and in every month only those shoots that have got to the desired length and that are going woody at the base should be pruned back. The end growths should not be pruned in this way. They should be cut back normally late in the winter.

RINGING

If a tree over nine or ten years of age is impossible to control by pruning, that is to say, if it is making a tremendous amount of wood and is not fruiting satisfactorily, it is possible to check growth effectively and force the tree into bearing by a process known as Ringing.

In April or May a ring of bark $\frac{1}{4}$ inch wide is removed right the way round the trunk of the tree. It mustn't be wider than this except in the case of very large trees or the check to growth may be too severe. Cover the ring thus made with adhesive tape. If adhesive tape is not available, paint the open wound with white lead paint. If it is impossible to treat the main trunk in this way each individual branch will have to be rung. This is a much simpler way of checking growth than root pruning, and on the whole is more effective.

SOFT FRUIT PRUNING

As for the pruning of black currants, gooseberries, raspberries, blackberries, etc., instructions will be found in detail in the chapters dealing with these fruits.

CHAPTER IV

THE TYPES OF TREES YOU CAN BUY

THERE is little difficulty in training fruit trees in different forms or shapes, and amateurs who learn to graft and bud their own trees find no difficulty in the long run in training these trees accordir.g to their own likes and dislikes. Beginners, on the other hand, always do well to buy their trees already trained by the nurserymen in the particular form they require them (and by the way, it is always worth while going to a reliable nurseryman and paying a fair price rather than buying a cheap lot because it is advertised in the Press.) Trees trained in special ways are always more expensive than those which are allowed to grow more naturally, and trees that have had to be in the Nursery for, say five years, while they are in the process of training, always feel the shock of transplanting far more than a two year old tree and therefore need greater care and attention.

THE BUSH

This is the simplest form for any beginner to have. It is a tree with a stem growing 2 ft. or so out of the ground and having branches evenly spaced. The nurseryman aims to produce an open goblet-shaped framework which should have six or seven good branches

HALF STANDARD

This is a tree with a stem about 4 ft. 6 inches from ground level. It is the type of tree often used by those who wish to plant in poultry runs. It is quite a suitable type of tree for planting in grass and is often used for plums and cooking apples.

25

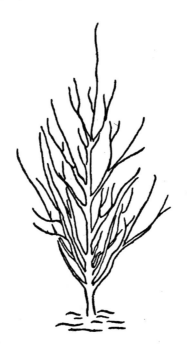

STANDARD

This tree has a stem 6 ft. or even 7 ft. above ground level and is not at all a suitable type for the small garden. It is a tree that is used in the orchard and its tall stem allows cattle to graze underneath without any fear of harm. The famous cherry orchards of Kent are planted with Standard cherries and the sheep graze underneath and keep the grass low.

The head of both the standard and half-standard tree is trained to start with in a similar manner to the bush tree.

THE FUSEAU, OR DWARF PYRAMID

This is a new type of tree that has come into fashion lately for both apples and pears. The tree is grown on a leg 30 inches tall, similarly to the bush. On the other hand instead of the branches being trained goblet or cup shaped, a central branch is allowed to grow as straight as possible and as this central branch is taken up and up side branches are allowed to grow out from it as per the diagram. Such trees are said to come into fruiting much earlier than the bushes but on the whole they are more difficult to prune and train. The aim is to have tiers of side branches growing out from the centre branch so that they develop spirally, tier above tier.

CORDONS

This is a very popular type of tree for the small garden owner, for it takes up the least amount of room. Apples, pears, gooseberries and red currants can be grown as cordons but this is not a suitable method for plums, cherries or black currants, all of which bear on the young wood. Cordons have to be trained along wires. They consist of single stemmed trees, the side growths of which are pruned back hard so that fruiting spurs develop the whole of their length. The trees are then planted in rows 2 ft. apart but trained at an angle of about 45

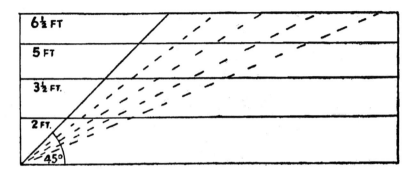

degrees against a fence or against a wire erection put up specially for the purpose. (See illustration.)

Cordons, if preferred may be trained horizontally so that they are running along wires stretched 1 ft. or so above ground level. They then make quite a good edging to a path. There are such things as double vertical cordons or even triple cordons. In this case instead of one stem being taken up, two or three stems are then trained instead in such a way as to run parallel to one another. Each stem in its turn is kept pruned back hard.

ESPALIER

The espalier is used for apples and pears as well as for red currants and goosberries. Espaliers are usually trained on walls or fences and the branches are spaced out so as to be 1 ft. apart and parallel one to the other. There may be three, four or even five tiers. The espalier tree will arrive from the nurseryman already trained and all the amateur has to do is to continue the pruning in the manner already done.

FAN TRAINED

As the espalier system is suited to the apple and pear so is the fan trained system for the stone fruits which bear on the young wood. In this system the trees are

trained just like a fan but every year it is possible to cut out some of the old wood and train some of the young wood in its place, provided the shape of the old fan is kept. (See the drawing above.)

CHAPTER V

WHEN TO PICK AND HOW TO STORE

WITH the soft fruits there is at the present time no question of storage, though of course, those with a Frigidaire will be able to keep their raspberries or strawberries for a number of days if necessary. The only other way of storing fruit successfully is by bottling or canning and any amateur can learn to preserve fruits in this way. In the case of canning there are comparatively cheap Home Canning plants available for the purpose.

Fruit picking time usually extends from June till early November. The actual times and dates vary from district to district. On the whole fruits have to be picked earlier in the South, for instance, than in the North. In addition it matters whether the fruit is to be picked because it is to be used immediately, and if so it should be fully ripe, whereas if it is to be picked for storing, it should be gathered just before fully ripe, and before it is fully mature. Fruits that are picked while immature, that is before they are fully grown, shrivel in storage and lose their flavour. It is quite easy to tell when any fruit is ready to pick for when ready the fruit stalk parts easily from the twig or spur on which it is growing. When the fruit is raised slightly.

Picking should always be done carefully and fruit should never be grasped with the thumb and forefinger. Even the slightest squeezing will cause bruises and a bruised fruit will not keep. Take the fruit in the palm of the hand, lift it slightly, and if it comes away easily, from the stem on which it is growing it is ready to gather.

Do not mix fallen fruit with picked fruit. Windfalls are always bruised and if mixed with specimens that have been carefully gathered will only lead to rotting and the damaged fruit will infect the sound specimens.

WHEN?

Pick the windfalls up immediately they are seen and use them as soon as possible. The longer they are kept the less valuable they will be.

Leave the late keeping fruit on the trees as long as possible, thus they will get to their largest size and best flavour.

Summer and autumn fruits should be picked just before they are absolutely ripe, except in the case of peaches and nectarines, which should not be gathered until just a day before they are fully ripe. Cherries are better gathered when ripe and not a day before.

Fruit that when gathered is found to be infected by insects or fungus diseases should not be stored with sound fruit but, as in the case of windfalls, should be used immediately.

How?

Having picked the fruits off carefully do not drop them into a container or they will bruise. Use a basket or better still, a smooth bucket, and put the fruits individually in these. By the way, if a basket is used, it is better to pad it, to prevent the ribbing of the wicker work rubbing the skins of the fruits and chafing them.

Never shake fruit off trees. Always use ladders or picking stools so as to climb up and be able to gather the fruit with ease. That is one of the great advantages of growing dwarf or bush trees, for then all the fruits can be picked without much ladder work.

From the pail or basket put the fruits into the box or tray in which they are going to be stored. The less fruit is handled, the better, and so whatever container is being used in the storehouse, carry out into the garden so that the fruit may be put into it right away, and thus prevent the fruit being placed in the bucket, from the bucket into, say, a barrow and then from the barrow to the storage tray. Handling soon removes the bloom off fruit, this particularly applies, of course, to pears, plums and peaches.

STORING—WHERE?

Too often there is no proper accommodation for storing fruit. A cock loft is not suitable because it heats up quickly and gets cold at night time, neither is an attic for the same reason. A garage is definitely unsuitable for the fumes of the petrol will infect the fruit. Fruit does not store well in any room with a wooden floor.

The A.R.P. dug-out on the other hand usually makes an ideal place for fruit storage for what is required is a dark, dry well-aired compartment underground. If it has to be above ground, a substantial outhouse will do, providing it is well insulated. It is possible to convert an outhouse into a fruit storage room at very little expense by thatching the roof and by fixing thick layers of straw around the inside of the walls to give the right insulation. Such a house should have ample ventilation so that on dry days the atmosphere can be changed if necessary.

The atmosphere of the storage room should be on the moist side. If it is too dry the fruit will shrivel; the temperature should be about 45 deg. F. all the time. It should be possible to give ample ventilation for the first three weeks after the fruit has been put into the store, to allow it to sweat. Inside the store room the fruit can be laid on shallow trays which can either slip into position like drawers or can be a fixture. If preferred orchard boxes (which may be bought made specially for the purpose) can be used these being stood one above the other. These boxes, because of the special method of construction, allow the air to circulate.

No house should be used that has been recently tarred or creosoted. No storehouse should be employed that has had paraffin in it, or even naphthalene or camphor.

Strong smells of any kind are quickly absorbed by stored fruit. The great thing is to have the storehouse water-proof as well as vermin proof. Rats and mice must be kept out at all costs.

WHAT TO DO

Having picked the fruits, only attempt to store those that really will keep. Be sure you don't put into the storehouse varieties that should be used right away. Once a fortnight go into the storehouse and look over the fruit carefully, removing any specimens that may have decayed before these contaminate the whole. This is particularly important in the case of pears which decay very rapidly.

If the storehouse has already got fruit in it and there is a later batch being picked, it is better to leave such fruit outside the store for a fortnight or three weeks after picking (covered over with an old tarpaulin) so that it may " sweat " there before being brought in close proximity to the other fruit.

Wrapping the fruits individually is a very good idea, especially if wrapping papers can be used which are previously treated with a flavourless mineral oil. Most Horticultural Sundriesmen offer these oiled wrapping papers for sale, and in 1940 they cost 4s. per 1,000. If, however, oiled wrapping paper is not avail-able, newspaper may be used instead. The advantage of wrapping is that the fruit keeps better and should one specimen break down, and start to rot, the paper will prevent it infecting another.

Some amateurs have used dried bracken leaves with great success. A layer of dried bracken leaves is placed on the floor or shelf and on this is put a layer of apples. Over the top is spread another layer of dried bracken leaves followed by another layer of apples, and so on. Straw should not be used for this curiously enough, imparts an unpleasant flavour to the fruit, whereas the dried bracken leaves do not.

CHAPTER VI

KEEPING THE PESTS AND DISEASES AWAY

UNFORTUNATELY there are all kinds of pests and diseases which attack fruit trees, bushes and canes. There are so many of them, in fact, that whole books have been written on the subject! The garden owner can, however, do much to prevent trouble by what may be called orchard hygiene, and everybody knows that prevention is better than cure! This chapter, therefore, will deal with the ways and means by which pests and diseases can be kept at bay and any specific measures that may be necessary will be found in the chapters dealing with the individual fruit.

SUN AND AIR

Do not plant your trees and bushes too close together. It is when they are overcrowded that predisposition to attacks of pests and diseases always occurs. Again, do not allow the trees and bushes themselves to grow overcrowded. See that the sunshine and air can get to all parts of the trees. If you take over a garden that is overcrowded, make it your first job to grub out every other tree or bush or whatever may be necessary. Keep the hedges well trimmed back.

REMOVAL OF INFECTION

Always cut out the dead branches immediately they are seen. Remove infected fruits, badly attacked leaves, in fact, cut away and burn diseased material so that the spores of the diseases cannot " breed " and develop, and so cause further infection. Be certain that the hedges are not causing infection. For instance, Wild Myrobelan

34

plum hedges are cause of diseases and pests reaching cultivated trees.   Where they have to be present it is well worth while spraying the hedges in the winter as well as the trees.   Try and get a neighbour to adopt control measures and you can often encourage him if you are willing to lend your spraying machine.   It is a pity to have your trees properly looked after, and then to be constantly getting infection from the trees next door.

CORRECT MANURING

Remember that if you do not manure your trees properly they may produce such an abundance of soft foliage that pests and diseases will come more readily. Aim at producing firm, dark green foliage that is not easily attacked.   Soft, luxuriant foliage always comes when heavy doses of nitrogen are given, either in an organic or inorganic form.   This is one of the reasons why it is undesirable to grow vegetable crops in between fruit trees and bushes because you may want to treat the vegetables liberally and the trees will get an overdose in consequence.   Remember that to check excessive leaf growth, potash must be used to balance.   Normally sulphate of potash will be used at 2-3 ounces to the square yard but if unobtainable, wood ashes may be applied instead at $\frac{1}{2}$ lb. to the square yard.   Always withhold nitrogenous manures completely when trying to rectify soft foliage conditions.

ENCOURAGE FRUIT FRIENDS

Remember that the ladybirds and their larvæ, those little black " crocodile-shaped " insects, known as " niggers " are very helpful for they feed almost entirely on green-fly.   Wasps, though they damage fruit, also feed on flies and grubs.   The Chalcid Wasp—that insect which seems to hover absolutely still in the path as you walk down, and is wasp-coloured, is also a friendly insect.   Rooks and owls and some other birds are also helpful in consuming pests. Poultry running beneath fruit trees will also help with pest control, but they never do the work sufficiently well to make spraying unnecessary.

Trapping To Kill

Greasebands of specially prepared grease which keeps tacky for months should be put around apple, pear and plum trees late in September or early in October for they prevent the wingless females of a large group of moths from crawling up the trunks and laying their eggs in the branches and spurs. Be sure to buy the best grease for the purpose for there are one or two cheaper types on the market which only keep sticky for a week or two. These greasebands will also help to trap the leaf-eating weevils, the woolly aphides, the capsid bugs, etc.

Bands of sacking may also be used tied round the trunks of the trees in order to trap the Codlin Moth caterpillar after it comes out of the apple, and crawls down the trunk of the tree. If a band of sacking is tied on the grub will hide in this and when the band is taken off in October the larvæ may be dropped into a little tin of paraffin. Fix the sacking band into position before the end of July. Corrugated cardboard bands will be on sale after the war, treated with Betanaphol. These, if tied on, have a dual function; they entice the larvæ to enter the corrugation where they are promptly killed by the chemical. A pest known as the Apple Blossom Weevil which ruins the blossoms of apples can also be trapped and killed by the sacking or corrugated cardboard band method.

Routine Washing And Spraying

Just as human beings need regular baths and washing, in order that they may be healthy and clean, so do fruit trees and bushes. It isn't a question of spraying when necessary. There are certain sprays and washes that must be put on each year as an insurance, come what may. The first main spraying is in the winter when all the leaves have fallen. The bare tree or bush must then be covered all over with a special wash which will kill as many of the insect eggs as possible that are laid on the trees; in addition a good winter wash should remove the moss and lichen and should give the whole tree a clean appearance.

Most growers use a tar oil, or what is called a Tar Distillate Wash and this can be bought under various proprietary names. The tar distillate wash is black when purchased but turns pure white when mixed with water. It will clean up the tree and kill the overwintering eggs of the apple sucker, the scale insects, the green fly and most eggs of the moths of the leaf-eating caterpillars. The tar oil wash, however, will not destroy the eggs of the capsid bugs and red spider. A new wash known as D.N.C. (Di-nitro-ortho-cresol) will kill the eggs of the capsid bugs and red spider as well as the others and so is much recommended. It is, however, bright yellow in colour, and does stain the skin and clothing. It is necessary, therefore, when using D.N.C. to smear the hands and face with vaseline, lanoline or similar material and to wear an old coat or mackintosh.

Winter washes have to be applied in such a manner that the tree is covered from top to toe. No little twig must be missed. It is a question of giving the trees a thorough soaking. The wash should be applied with as much pressure as possible but the A.R.P. Stirrup Pumps are very useful for this purpose as are hand spraying machines, such as the Solo Sprayer, which can be purchased expressly for spraying.

Having applied the winter wash to clean up the tree, it is necessary, at any rate, with apples and pears, to use a lime-sulphur or colloidal wash as a cover to prevent attacks of fungus diseases which are carried about on the wind or by insects. When the spore of a disease falls on a leaf it starts to send out is delicate " root," but if the leaf has been covered with a fungicide the spore is killed before it starts to grow. Lime-sulphur is the commonest fungicide used at the moment and this is usually employed at the rate of 1 pint to 30 pints of water just before the blossoms open, and at the rate of 1 pint to 60-80 pints of water, immediately after the blossoms have fallen. In the second lime-sulphur spraying, nicotine can be added which will help to kill any insects that may be about at the time particularly those of the apple sawfly, the second of those pests that causes maggots in the apples (the other one you will remember from the earlier reading, is the codlin moth).

SPREADERS AND WETTERS

In order to ensure that the spray used covers the maximum area in the minimum of time, substances known as spreaders or wetters are used. The commonest spreader is soft soap. It enables an insecticide to penetrate among the foliage and is usually used with nicotine for this reason. Soft soap cannot however be used with lime-sulphur but there are proprietary spreaders to be bought such as Estol H. The spreader does ensur that the lime-sulphur is evenly distributed all over the leaf and doesn't just go on in blobs. Use proprietary spreaders in accordance with the makers' instructions.

DRY SPRAYS

Dusting is sometimes used instead of spraying. It is useless in the winter time but it is quite convenient in the spring and summer. Dust can be applied much more quickly than liquid sprays and of course they save all the bother of carting water. Dusting machines of all kinds can now be bought, the Rotary Fan Dust Gun is obviously the best tool at the moment. Among the dusts that can be used are the Nicotine dusts for controlling insects and the Sulphur dusts for controlling fungus diseases. Derris Dust is very useful too, for it isn't poisonous and yet gives good insect control. Dust should always be applied when there is little wind about or the specific may drift for miles. Dusts on the whole are more easily washed off by rain than sprays.

CHAPTER VII

GROWING DESSERT AND COOKING APPLES

THERE is every excuse for growing apples in this country for they grow better here than anywhere else. New Zealand, perhaps, comes a very good second but those who have travelled all over the world say, again and again, that English apples are best, and that goes for Scotland and Ireland too! At any rate it is the most grown fruit in England and probably the longest grown.

Apples may be roughly divided into four classes: the Crab apples, which are usually grown for their beauty rather than for their value, though of course they make delicious Crab apple jelly. The Cider apples which are generally grown in the South-West of England in grass orchards and which themselves can be classified into sour, sweets, bitter-sweets and so on. The dessert apple which is always eaten in great quantities and the cooking apple which finds its way into the pies, the tarts, the dumplings, the apple charlotte, and the innumerable dishes in which the English housewife excels.

SOIL AND SITUATION

Apples don't like badly drained soils and they dislike those that dry out in a hot summer. Apple fruits do not keep well if they are grown on land which has been heavily manured in the past or in the present, that is why the apple trees planted in kitchen gardens usually grow large but are not good keepers. Where you have to use kitchen gardens for apple planting put in cookers rather than dessert varieties, or where it is necessary to plant trees in a light, dry, sandy soil, use dessert varieties and prepare to be generous with potash manures.

Those who live in the wetter parts of England, the

West and North-West, will find that cooking apples do best with them. Those who live in the drier parts, *i.e.,* the East and South-East, will find dessert varieties ideal. This doesn't mean to say that both types could not be grown in these two differing areas but the ideal conditions have been mentioned. It has been stated, for instance, that the best dessert apples can be produced in gardens where the rainfall is from 20-25 inches per year and where there is a high rate of sunshine. Where the rainfall exceeds 40 inches a year dessert apples are certainly difficult to grow.

Trees To Buy

For planting in a lawn or in a grass orchard the half-standard or the standard will be best. The same rules apply when planting in a poultry run. For the ordinary garden the bush tree is undoubtedly the most useful, while when there are certain restrictions of space, particularly in a lateral direction, the dwarf pyramid is to be preferred. Those who have little room should plant cordons and train them either along the fences or walls or up wire stretched between posts; for distances apart, see Chapter IV.

The Root Stock

Far more important than even variety or type of tree is the root stock on which the tree is grafted or budded. It is the root stock which determines whether the tree is to grow strongly, whether it is going to crop during the first few years or whether no fruit is going to appear for ten years or so. When ordering fruit trees it is most important to insist that they be " worked " on Malling root stocks which have been numbered for the purpose.

For the small garden there is nothing better than Malling 9. It prevents the tree growing too large; it causes the variety to crop early. It produces fruits of large size and high colour. Trees grafted on No. 9

remain through their lives smaller than trees grafted on any other root stock.

For the standard or half-standard tree a much stronger type of stock is required and therefore Malling No. 12 or No. 16 should be used. These take a number of years before they bring the variety into bearing but they give trees with nice large heads. For the medium sized tree there is much to recommend Malling 2, which can be used by those who need large bush trees or who want to encourage a very dwarfing variety into stronger growth.

It cannot be over-emphasized that all trees should be bought from a Nurseryman who can guarantee the number of the stock on which they are grafted. Normally the garden owner should stick to Malling No. 9.

Pruning Hints

General remarks on Pruning will be found in Chapter III.

It will only be necessary here, therefore, to give special pruning hints which apply mainly to apples only. The winter pruning of apples is normally done during the second half of November and during the whole of December. It is a good plan to get the winter pruning over before the tar distillate winter washing is done as this economises in the amount of spray fluid required.

The stronger varieties of apples like Bramley Seedling and Newton Wonder are best not pruned after the first few years, and all that need be done each winter is to cut out dead, and dying wood, and interlacing branches. The less strong growing varieties like Early Victoria, James Grieve, Cox's Orange Pippin, and Lord Derby, are usually pruned every year by cutting back the one year old side growths, or laterals, to within three buds of their base, and by reducing the leaders, or end one year old growths by about half. This causes the large proportion of fruit buds to be developed on the shortened lateral shoots.

There are varieties, however, like Irish Peach, Barnack Beauty, Lord Gladstone and Grenadier, Bismarck and Worcester Pearmain which produce their fruit buds at the end of thin twiggy side shoots. It is therefore necessary to leave the laterals of these varieties long. They are usually known as tip bearers, that is to say they bear on the tips of the growths. With these varieties the leaders are cut back by half but the laterals are not pruned back till three or four years afterwards when fruit buds will have developed nearer their base.

Watch the growth of the variety carefully. Some like Edward VII and King of the Pippins tend to grow upright. In cases like these always cut the leaders just above an outward pointing bud. Others, like Lane's Prince Albert, Stirling Castle and Gladstone, tend to spread too much. The leaders of these should always be pruned to just above an upward pointing bud so as to keep them upright.

MANURING HINTS

Try and give apples the nitrogen and potash they require in accordance with their needs. The apples growing in grass will need mainly nitrogen only. The apples on the other hand in cultivated land will generally require potash only. Cooking apples require more nitrogen than dessert apples. Dessert apples need more potash than cooking apples. It would be a good plan to give dessert apples 2 ounces of sulphate of potash per square yard each November or December, or twice the quantity of wood ashes instead. Cooking apples should receive in addition 1 ounce of sulphate of ammonia in January per square yard. If the cooking apples were growing in grass two dressings of sulphate of ammonia or nitro-chalk should be given, the first in February and the second in May; in both cases 1 ounce to the square yard.

ROUTINE WORK

The general routine in an apple orchard should be roughly as follows :

NOVEMBER-DECEMBER
Pruning trees, burning diseased wood, painting cuts.

DECEMBER
Spraying trees with tar distillate wash or D.N.C.

JANUARY
Applying fertilisers required, *i.e.*, nitrogen or potash, or both.

SPRING
Spraying trees with a fungicide, usually lime-sulphur just before the blossoms open, and just after the blossoms open. Other sprayings may be necessary to control insect pests such as Apple Sawfly, Codlin Moth caterpillars, etc.

JUNE-JULY
Thinning fruits if there is a heavy crop. See page

SUMMER-AUTUMN
Picking fruits and storing.

SEPTEMBER-OCTOBER
Applying grease bands to catch wingless moths, etc.

NOTES ON WORK :

    (*a*) Thinning :   To get good sized fruits it is necessary to thin in June and July to 8 ins. apart. This also ensures more regular cropping. When thinning always remove the centre fruit of of each truss because this is always abnormal.

    (*b*) Picking :   Early ripening varieties can be picked as required. Later varieties should be picked when the apple will come away from the twig or spur without an effort. If the stalk has to be torn off the apple may not keep well. Handle apples very carefully. They bruise very easily. Always pick when they are quite dry.

    (c) Greasebands : See Chapter VI.

APPLE VARIETIES

There are hundreds of varieties of apples and to describe them in detail in a book of this size would be

impossible. There will be found below a number of
lists of apples carefully compiled with the object of trying
to suit varying needs.

BEST EATING APPLES FOR SMALL GARDEN

Charles Ross	Cox's Orange Pippin
Epicure	Ellison's Orange
Fortune	James Grieve
Laxton's Exquisite	Laxton's Superb
Rival	St. Cecelia

BEST COOKING APPLES FOR SMALL GARDENS

Arthur Turner	Early Victoria
Edward VII	Grenadier
Lane's Prince Albert	Lord Derby
Monarch	The Rev. W. Wilks

BEST APPLES FOR WALLS AND FENCES

NORTH WALL	SOUTH WALL
Beauty of Bath	James Grieve
James Grieve	Laxton's Superb
Worcester Pearmain	Cox's Orange Pippin

EAST WALL	WEST WALL
Beauty of Bath	Ellisons Orange
Ellison's Orange	James Grieve
James Grieve	Laxton Superb
Laxton's Superb	Lady Sudeley

Most early cookers will grow well on any of these walls.

FOR VERY LARGE APPLES

DESSERT	CULINARY
Charles Ross	Peasgood's Nonsuch
Peacemaker	Rev. W. Wilks
King of Tomkins County	Bramley Seedling
	Mere de Menage

BRILLIANTLY COLOURED APPLES

DESSERT	CULINARY
Crimson Cox	Emperor Alexander
Crimson Newton	Early Red Victoria
Gascoigne's Scarlet	Crimson Bramley
John Standish	
Laxton's Early Crimson	
Red Coat Grieve (Rosamund)	

NICEST FLAVOURED DESSERT APPLES

VARIETY	SEASON
Blenheim Orange	December
Cornish Gillyflower	December-March

Cox's Orange Pippin	December-January
D'Arcy Spice	March-May
Irish Peach	September
Laxton's Exquisite	September
Laxton's Superb	January-March
American Mother	End of October
Owen Thomas	August
Ribston Pippin	November
Rosemary Russet	February

BRIEF LIST—ORDER OF RIPENING

EATING	COOKING
Irish Peach	Arthur Turner
Lady Sudeley	Early Victoria
Miller's Seedling	Grenadier
Mr. Gladstone	Golden Noble
Worcester Pearmain	Lord Derby
James Grieve	Rev. W. Wilks
Laxton's Exquisite	Lane's Prince Albert
Charles Ross	Encore
Ellison's Orange	Monarch
Cox's Orange Pippin	Newton Wonder
Laxton's Superb	Bramley Seedling

PESTS AND DISEASES.   *Practical Points.*

Caterpillars (various). These develop from eggs laid by different types of moths. They eat the leaves and/or the flowers. They may not only ruin a crop for one year but so devitalise a tree as to prevent it being able to crop the following year. Answer: Apply the greasebands as advised Early October. Spray each winter with a good tar distillate wash.

Green Flies (aphides). Various kinds of aphides which suck the leaves, suck the young growths, curl the leaves, attack the newly formed fruits, causing them to become knobbly. Answer: Spray the trees each December with a good tar distillate wash to kill the eggs.

American Blight (Woolly Aphis). Cotton-wool-like substance found on the branches and twigs. May kill young growth. May introduce canker. Will cause "galls" on branches. Answer: Spray D.N.C. in December. Paint affected parts with strong liquid Derris in summer when seen.

. Capsid Bug. Little green aphid-like insects which move very rapidly. At first they have no wings. Then they grow in size and develop wings, flying thus from tree to tree. These bugs produce corky scars on the fruits, often distorting them. They also feed on the new shoots, causing these to branch out. Answer: Spray the trees thoroughly with D.N.C. in December. Spray with strong nicotine in the summer.

Maggots in Apple (A), Apple Sawfly: (B) *Codlin Moth.* The maggot of the Sawfly is a dirty white with a brown head and can be distinguished from the maggot of the codlin moth by the quantity of frass it exudes. If damaged it smells badly. The sawfly maggot attack is much earlier than that of the codlin moth maggot. The codlin moth maggot is pale pink with a brown head. Answer: If Sawfly, spray immediately the petals have fallen, with nicotine, 1 oz. to 10 gallons water. If codlin, spray late in June with arsenate of lead, and again in mid-July. Formula, ¼ lb. lead arsenate paste to 6 gallons water.

Other pests. There are many other pests such as the Leaf Eating Weevils, The Scale insects, the big caterpillars which burrow into the trunks of the trees, and so on, but the routine sprayings already mentioned should prevent much trouble.

Scab. Black spots occur on the apples. These spots may spread and look like huge scabs. Later they may crack. Answer: Spraying with lime-sulphur just before the blossoms open and just after the blossoms have fallen; at the pre-blossom at 1 pint to 30 pints water and at the post blossom stage at 1 pint to 60 pints water.

Canker. A disease which eats into the wood of the tree, causing sunken discoloured, degenerating tissue. A bad canker may girdle a whole branch. Answer: Cut out the cankers with a sharp knife directly they are seen and paint with Medo.

Brown Rot. The apple goes brown and rotten. The disease may occur while the fruits are still on the trees, or after they have been picked. Spores usually enter through a wound made by a bird-peck, an insect puncture, a crack caused by Scab, or a bruise caused by picking. Answer: Pick all affected fruits immediately they are seen, and burn them. Spray trees in December with a tar distillate wash and in the January following, with caustic soda, formula 2 lbs. caustic soda to 10 gallons water.

Mildew. The shoots and leaves seem to have a white powdery, mealy dust on them. The disease is wind borne. Answer: Cut off and burn all infected shoots and leaves. Spray with lime-sulphur as for Scab.

CHAPTER VIII

GROWING DESSERT AND COOKING CHERRIES

CHERRIES are grown in all parts of the country but principally in Kent, Buckingham and Hereford. It is said they were first planted in Great Britain in A.D. 100, but the big Kent industry didn't start till about 1540.

The Morello or sour cherry is quite different from the sweet cherry, and is often grown in bush form. The sweet cherry isn't a very suitable fruit for growing in a small garden because it takes up a great deal of room, and further, it is so difficult to keep the birds away and thus little fruit is ever harvested. Where cherry growing is to be carried out in a garden it is best done on walls or fences.

SOIL AND SITUATION

Cherries undoubtedly do best on land which is deep and well drained and where the rainfall is moderately light. They dislike heavy wet soils as well as light soils which dry out in the fruiting season. It is most important during blossoming time to provide cherries with shelter from the East Winds and as cherry flowers are very susceptible to frost, protection has to be given as a rule when the flowers are out. The best walls or fences for cherries are those which face South or West. Morello cherries, i.e., sour cherries, will grow quite well on a North or East wall.

TREES TO BUY

Morellos may be purchased as bush trees and the sweet cherries for the grass orchard as standards. In the garden sweet cherries should be grown as fan trained trees or as cordons.

ROOT STOCKS

It is very difficult to keep a wall cherry confined because no really dwarfing root stocks for cherries have yet been found. The usual stock for the standard sweet cherry is the Mazzard, or Wild Cherry, and this is quite a suitable stock for the acid or Morello cherries also.

PRUNING HINTS

Once the cherry tree has been formed the less it is pruned the better. In fact with standard trees it is advisable to cut out only the dead and crossing branches in August as during this month the spores of the Silver Leaf fungus are not active.

Wall trees of sweet cherries should be summer pruned by cutting back the laterals growing away from the wall to within five buds of their base in July, and further still to within three buds of their base in September. When the tree gets to the top of the wall do not keep cutting back the end growths but allow them to grow naturally for a year or two when it will be possible to cut back to a flowering shoot lower down.

Sour cherries should be pruned differently from the sweet cherries above, because these bear on the young growth. The object, therefore, is to cut out some old growth each season and to retain the new.

MANURING HINTS

Wall trees should not be given nitrogen until they are bearing heavy crops regularly, for they tend to make too much shoot growth normally. Once a heavy crop has set, a good mulching of rotted vegetable refuse should be spread on the surface of the ground around the stem for several feet.

Each November give superphosphate at 3 ounces

to the square yard and potash at 1 ounce to the square yard. When the trees are in full bearing, apply sulphate of ammonia in January at 1 ounce to the square yard. Lime should be given every four years at the rate of 5 ounces of hydrated lime per square yard. Mulchings with rotted vegetble refuse should always be applied to wall trees as advised above.

WATERING

If the weather is dry during June and July it will be necessary to give thorough waterings to wall trees.

ROUTINE WORK

NOVEMBER-DECEMBER
Pruning, burning diseased wood, painting cuts with thick white lead paint.

DECEMBER
Spraying trees with Tar distillate wash or D.N.C.

JANUARY
Applying fertilisers not given in November.

JUNE AND JULY
Watering if necessary.

SUMMER
Picking fruits and protecting against birds.

AUGUST
Cutting out dead wood and crossing branches.

NOTES ON ROUTINE WORK.
(a) Picking. Always pick cherries when dry. Early varieties like Early Rivers in June and late varieties mid-August. Gather with the stalks: don't handle the cherries. Go over trees two or three times removing cherries that are ripe. It is convenient to cut off Morello cherries with scissors.

CHERRY VARIETIES

It is most important to remember that all sweet cherries need pollinators and therefore it is necessary to plant pairs in every case. Morello cherries can pollinate themselves.

BEST EATING CHERRIES FOR SMALL GARDEN, WITH
POLLINATORS.

Early Rivers, a black	Pollinator	Governor Wood
Frogmore, a white	„	Roundel
Elton Heart, a white	„	Noire de Guben
Governor Wood, a white	„	Early Rivers
Black Eagle, a black	Bigarreau	Schrecken
Waterloo, a black	„	Napoleon
Bradbourne Black, black	„	Napoleon
Napoleon, a white	„	Waterloo
Noble	„	Napoleon

This list has been designed to provide cherries from the
end of June to the beginning of August. The varieties
are placed in the order of earliness.

SOUR CHERRIES.   In order of ripening.

May Duke, end June.	Arch Duke, early July.
Kentish Red, mid-July.	Flemish Red, end July.
Morello, end July.	Late Duke, early August.

BEST VARIETIES FOR WALLS.

NORTH	SOUTH	EAST	WEST
Kentish Red.	Napoleon.	Napoleon.	Napoleon.
May Duke.	Black Eagle.	Early Rivers.	Early Rivers.
Morello.	Early Rivers.	Governor Wood.	Governor Wood.
	Elton.	Morello.	Black Eagle.
	Florence.		
	Frogmore.		

PESTS AND DISEASES

If routine tar distillate wash or D.N.C. sprayings are
carried out cherries should give little trouble.

Caterpillars.   Eat the leaves, blossoms, and ruin the crop.
Answer: A thorough spraying in December with a tar oil
wash.   If omitted, spray immediately caterpillars seen with
arsenate of lead.

Black Fly. (Aphides).   This is similar to the black aphides
seen on broad beans.   It attacks the young shoots and leaves
and may kill them.   Answer: Spray with good tar oil wash in
December; spray in summer in case of secondary attack, with
nicotine and soft soap.

Leaf Scorch.   The leaves do not fall in the autumn but
remain dead on the tree throughout the winter.   Answer:
Strip the leaves from the trees in winter and burn them.
Spray immediately after the blossoming period with Bordeaux
Mixture to prevent new leaves being infected.

D

Chapter IX

CURRANTS OF ALL KINDS

Currants must be classified in the first place into two big classes—the black currants and the red and white currants. Though they are all currants, there is almost every difference possible between the red and white, and the black. Black currants, for instance, bear on the new wood; red and white currants bear on short spurs on the old wood. Black currants like lots of nitrogen. Red and white currants seek after potash. It is true that there are many diseases in common and many pests too, but it is important to remember that these two main groups of currants differ so much in their demands that they are better planted apart. Black currants on one side of the path, for instance, and red and white on the other.

It is wondered whether white currants have any really important part to play. They are not particularly well flavoured and they make a poor type of jam or jelly alone. They are interesting when mixed in a fruit salad with the other types of currants and they have the advantage of being very heavy croppers as a rule. In most gardens, however, one or two bushes of white currants are ample.

BLACK CURRANTS
Soil and Situation
The black currant will do quite well on the heavy soil. It likes lots of organic matter and plenty of nitrogen. In order that the blossoms may set properly it is important to have insect visitors. Therefore black currants always ask for shelter from East and North winds during blossoming time. Insects will not work properly in a

windswept situation. Remember that a black currant bush will crop from two years old, as a rule, but it won't go on cropping satisfactorily unless it is properly fed and regularly sprayed. Black currant bushes when properly looked after will crop for ten years.

BUSHES TO BUY

Purchase two year old black currant bushes which should have their branches growing straight out of the ground. It is not advisable to have the bushes on a leg or stem. The heaviest crops result when the shoots develop from the base of the bush and even from buds below ground level. Never try and grow black currants in any trained form. They bear on the new wood and if you have to keep pruning the new wood back you get very little crop. Ban, therefore, artificial forms of black currants.

HOW TO PROPAGATE

Cuttings should be made from well-ripened one year old pieces of wood. These should only be taken from perfectly healthy bushes free from the Big Bud Mite and from the Reversion disease. Cut off the young wood that is to be used for cuttings in October and prepare them so that they are about 9 inches long. They should be cut just below a bud at the base of the cutting and just above a bud at its apex. No side buds should be removed. Such a cutting should be inserted in the ground in such a manner that only two buds are left above ground level. Cuttings always strike best in very sandy soil. Keep the rows of cuttings well hoed during the summer and the result should be good plants that can be put out into their permanent position the following winter.

PRUNING HINTS

When the new bush is put out into its permanent position all shoots should be cut down to within 2 inches of soil level. This will encourage strong growth in the future which will crop heavily the following year. After this, the plan should be to cut away a third of the bush each winter. By doing this strong young growth will be encouraged with the result that the cropping capacity of the bush will be maintained year after year.

Black currants should not be summer pruned for it is the young growths that are going to provide the fruiting wood for next season.

MANURING HINTS

See that the black currants are given sufficient nitrogen in the form of sulphate of ammonia or nitro-chalk. Each year these should be applied at about 2 ounces to the yard run along the rows in March. In addition Mulch the rows with whatever organic matter is available; animal dung if possible; pig dung is often used and is excellent for the purpose. Rotted vegetable refuse is also first-class. Such organic matter should be applied along the rows in November to be dug in and a further dressing may be given early in June to act as a mulch. For fear of lack of potash, a dressing of wood ashes at 3-4 ounces to the square yard is often given or sulphate of potash at about ½ ounce per square yard instead. The great thing, however, is to give black currants plenty of organic matter and ample nitrogen.

ROUTINE WORK

Herewith the principal jobs that have to be done with black currants.

NOVEMBER
Prune out the old wood, cutting away one third of the bush.

DECEMBER
Spray with a good tar distillate wash, or D.N.C. to control eggs and clean the bushes.

MARCH
Apply the artificial manures.

APRIL-MAY

See that the bushes are sprayed with lime-sulphur at 1 pint to 25 pints water just before the blossoms open and when the majority of the leaves are about the size of a two shilling piece. This is the only way of killing the Big Bud mite.

JUNE

Apply a good mulching of farmyard manure or well-rotted vegetable refuse along the rows.

SUMMER

Pick the fruit.

Notes on Routine Work

(a) Picking: It is a good plan to go over the bushes and pick the ripest berries first. Always pick in the early part of the day if possible and never pick during rain. Pick the berries by the strig when they are really black and it is usual to wait for two or three days, even after they have turned black if the berry is required fully ripe.

Varieties

Black currants can be divided up into various groups. There is the French group, for instance, that is perhaps the most widely planted. There is the Boskoop Group which is one of the earliest; there is the Goliath Group which grows a big bush; there is the Baldwin Group which grows a weak compact bush but produces the heaviest crops over a period of years, and there is the Intermediate Group which may be said to be a cross between the Baldwin and Boskoop types.

Those who want a large berry should plant the Boskoop, remembering that it must be sheltered or the flowers will not set. Those who want a heavy cropper will probably go in for Baldwin, while those who want a late variety will grow Daniel's Late September. Brief descriptions of the best varieties and the Group into which they fall will be found on next page.

Variety	Group	Growth	Season	Remarks
Baldwin	Baldwin	Compact, weak	Latish	Medium truss, skin of fruit tough. Hangs late.
Edina	Goliath	Compact	Mid season	Fruit large, sweet, skin tender. Sulphur shy and susceptible to aphis.
Daniel's September	Baldwin	F. vigorous	Very late	Skin of fruit tough.
Seabrook's Black	French	Vigorous, compact	Mid	Fruit medium, skin tough.
Boskoop Giant	Boskoop	Vigorous, drooping	Early	Long truss, large fruit sweet, needs shelter.
Goliath	Goliath	Compact	Mid	Fruit very large and sweet. Sulphur shy.
Wellington XXX	Intermediate	Vigorous, drooping	Early to Mid	Long truss, large sweet fruit.
Westwick Triumph	Intermediate	Vigorous, late		Truss long, fruit large, good variety.

SELECTION FOR SMALL GARDEN

Boskoop Giant.   Seabrooks Black.   Baldwin's Black.
Westwick Triumph.   Daniel's Late September.

RED CURRANTS, WHITE CURRANTS

As has already been suggested, very few white currants
will be needed—one or two at the most are ample in the
ordinary garden. Red currants are not as valuable as
black currants. They are useful for red currant jelly and
they make a good jam when mixed with raspberries. Few
people eat them alone for dessert, though those who do
like to eat them raw are very fond of them.

SOIL AND SITUATION

These currants seem to prefer plenty of sunlight to
any special type of soil. They will do well on heavy
lands and crop quite successfully on light soils. If they
do prefer one soil more than another it is one that is deep
and of medium texture. Always plant red currants in a
sheltered situation as the side shoots tend to break off in
the wind, especially with certain varieties. Red currants
should start to bear when three years of age and if they
are carefully looked after they will last for fifteen to
twenty years.

BUSHES TO BUY

Always buy red or white currants on a leg. The
stem should be 1 ft. or 18 inches long and you should
aim at eight good branches developing from the end of
the stem so as to form a bush shaped like a vase.

Red and white currants make good cordons and you
can train them along North or East walls or on wires in
the open. Red currants can be grown as espaliers.

Another excellent form for red currants is the half-
standard. When properly trained even the stem of the
red currant will bear fruit in addition to the branches.
The tree is therefore a beautiful sight when cropping,

the bunches of fruit hanging in profusion right the way up the trunk and from the branches also.

How to Propagate

Cuttings should be made of one year old wood soon after leaf-fall as possible in the late autumn. The cuttings should be 15 inches long if possible, a cut being made just below a bud at the base of the cutting and just above a bud at the tip. All the buds should be carefully cut away except the top three. The cutting should then be inserted 6 inches deep. One of the simplest ways of doing this is to fork the soil over to a depth of a spade and then to dig out a narrow trench 6 inches deep and push the cutting down vertically in this. Fill the trench half full and then tread the soil in firmly around the base of the cutting. Fill in the remainder of the trench and tread again.

Space the cuttings themselves 6 inches apart in the rows and have the cuttings 2 ft. apart between the rows. Leave the cuttings in position for two years and then transplant into their permanent place, or transplant at the end of one year, 12 inches square, replanting again at the end of the next year, 5 ft. apart.

Pruning Hints

Train the two-year old into a cup-shaped bush tree. Do this by pruning the lateral shoots back to within 1 inch and the end shoots or leaders cut back by about three-quarters to just above an outward pointing bud. Next winter do the same thing. Cut back the laterals not required to within 1 inch of their base and cut back the leaders or end growths by about half once more to just above an outside pointing bud. Aim in this way at selecting and developing eight or nine leading branches per bush. Any suckers coming up from the roots should be cut out.

In the summer all the side shoots (but not the leaders)

should be cut back to within five or six leaves of their base. This is to let the sunshine and air into the tree. Following this these growths will be cut back to within $\frac{1}{2}$ inch of their base in the winter and in the winter also, usually in December, the leading shoots or end growths will be shortened by one half, taking care to make the cuts just above a healthy bud.

Sometimes birds are nuisance and come to peck out the buds in the spring just before they are starting to break. Such bird damage can be prevented if the bushes are thickly cottoned with black cotton.

With Laxton's Perfection and Fay's Prolific there is a danger that the leaders may be " blown off " during the summer. This is due to the brittleness of the wood. It may be necessary, therefore, to support the branches in some way with bamboos.

MANURING HINTS

Every November or early December apply sulphate of potash at 1 or 2 ounces to the square yard or if this is not available, use wood ashes at $\frac{1}{2}$ lb to the square yard.

Give organic manure such as farmyard manure, pig manure or well composted vegetable refuse early in June each year at the rate of two good bucketfuls per bush. This top dressing should be worked into the ground in the winter.

ROUTINE WORK

Some of the routine work has been mentioned under the heading of Pruning. Please, therefore, study this section carefully.

NOVEMBER
Get all the winter pruning done and see that any diseased wood is burnt.

DECEMBER
Spray all the bushes with a good tar distillate wash or with D.N.C. to kill the eggs of pests and clean the bark of pests and lichen.

JANUARY
Apply sulphate of potash.

FEBRUARY-MARCH
Black Cotton the bushes to keep away birds.

JUNE
Give support to brittle varieties and give mulchings of organic matter around each bush.

SUMMER
Pick carefully, gathering the ripest first. Always pick with a strig and not by the berry. Pick early in the morning if possible, but never pick when the berries are wet if it can be helped.

VARIETIES

There are large numbers of red currant varieties but the following Chart gives details of the best few.

RED CURRANTS

VARIETIES	COLOUR	SIZE	SEASON	REMARKS
Comet	Crimson	Large	Aug.-Sept.	Not so acid as others.
Fay's Prolific	Deep red	Very large	Earlish	Long truss. Needs wind protection.
Versailles	Bright red	Very large	Mid season	One of the best. Needs protection.
Dutch	Dull red	Large	Latish	Good cropper.
Raby Castle	Bright red	Medium	Late	Good for cordons.
Earliest of Forland	Pale red	Medium	Early	Strong upright grower.
Prince Albert	Pale red	Medium	Very late	Perhaps the best late.
Laxton's Perfection	Dark red	Very large	Latish	Very long truss. Good for show.
Laxton's No. 1	Scarlet	Large	Mid season	Excellent.

WHITE CURRANTS

VARIETIES	COLOUR	SIZE	SEASON	REMARKS
Transparent	Yellowy-white	Large	Late	Long truss. Good for show.
Wentworth	Deep yellow	Large	Very late	Strong grower.
White Versailles	Pale yellow	Large	Early	Very sweet.

PESTS AND DISEASES. *Practical points.*

Big Bud. (Black Currant Mite.) This Mite attacks the buds of the bushes which swell and swell till they are five or six times their normal size and instead of being pointed are round. Answer: Spray the bushes with lime-sulphur, 1 pint to 25 pints of water when the flower racemes are seen but before the blossoms open. This is usually when the majority of the leaves are the size of a two shilling piece.

Green Flies (Aphides). These insects cause reddish coloured blisters on the leaves in the summer or they may curl the end leaves of the young shoot. Answer: Spray the bushes with a good tar distillate wash in December. If a second attack occurs in the summer, spray with nicotine and soft soap.

Caterpillars. Various types of caterpillars will eat the leaves. Answer: Directly they are seen spray with Liquid Derris.

Capsid Bug. Small brown spots will be found on the young leaves. In bad cases these become distorted and torn. The end shoots may be stunted or killed and excessive side branching may result. Answer: Spray with D.N.C. in December.

Leaf Spot. Numerous small brownish spots will be found on the upper surface of the leaves. These may merge together. Leaves often wither and fall in August. Answer: Spray with Bordeaux Mixture immediately the crop has been gathered.

Rust. The leaves, particularly the underside, will be covered with orange rusty spots, sometimes the leaves being so badly attacked that they will fall prematurely. Answer: Spray with Bordeaux Mixture immediately the crop has been picked.

Reversion. A very serious disease of black currants. Reverted leaves grow longer in shape, more like nettle leaves. Reverted blossoms seldom set fruit. When shape of leaves on bushes tend to elongate, suspect reversion and send samples to an expert. Answer: Reverted bushes must be dug up and burned immediately.

CHAPTER X

DESSERT AND COOKING GOOSEBERRIES

THE gooseberry belongs to the same family as the currant and may be attacked by similar diseases and pests. For instance, the Big Bud Mite which affects the black currant often attacks the gooseberry and instead of causing the bud to become enlarged remains the same size, but dies. They are probably the easiest soft fruits to grow, and the two main troubles that affect them in private gardens are mildew and the sawfly caterpillar. Fortunately keen gardeners will easily keep these two troubles away.

SOIL AND SITUATION

Gooseberries cannot stand bad drainage. Never plant them, therefore, in a garden that tends to be waterlogged. They will not grow properly unless they are given ample supplies of potash. That is why they do not do well in sandy soils unless these are properly fed. The best results are achieved when the bushes are planted in a deep well-drained, deeply dug loam, and are given the chance of having plenty of air and sunshine. Gooseberry bushes grown under these conditions have been known to crop profitably for fifteen years.

BUSHES TO BUY

Normally buy a goosberry bush on a short stem or leg. Never buy a bush whose branches grow straight out of the ground. One of the curses of the gooseberry bush is suckers coming up from the roots, but bushes on a leg that have been properly propagated seldom give this trouble.

Gooseberries do quite well as cordons or as espaliers.

They can be trained as half-standards if desired and then they will crop up the stems as well as along the branches. The dessert varieties are usually grown as cordons and espaliers, though of course they do equally well as bushes. It is seldom that cooking varieties are trained as cordons.

How to Propagate

Choose well ripened one year old wood about the end of October. Make the cuttings 15-18 inches long if possible, and with the sharp blade of a knife prepare by cutting the wood just below a bud at the base and just above a bud at the other end. Insert the cutting the right way up into the ground 6 or 7 inches deep. As in the case of red currants remove all the lower buds of the cutting so as to obviate any suckering and just leave the three or four buds at the top of the cutting to form the branches.

Fork the ground over a spade's depth. Take out little trenches 6 inches deep and lay the cuttings in these, upright 6 inches apart. Put back the soil and tread down very firmly. The best cuttings always result from firm soil. If the land is heavy, mix sand in with the soil, especially towards the base of the trench. After a year, when the cuttings should have developed three little branches they should be planted 1 ft. square into a nursery bed. The year after that they can be put out into their permanent positions.

Pruning Hints

If it is proposed to grow gooseberries as double cordons, cordons, espaliers or half-standards, it is advisable to purchase them already trained in one of these forms from the nurserymen and then there will be little difficulty in following the pruning already done, and so keeping to the shape of the trees.

There are two main ways of pruning ordinary bushes.

The first aims at getting quantity and the second at
quality. The first is simple, and entails very little work,
the second is more complicated and takes a fair amount
of time.

QUALITY METHOD

Keep the number of branches limited to seven or
eight. Cut back the lateral growths to within 2 inches
of their base each winter and prune back the end growth
or leader by about half, to just above an outward or
inward pointing bud, depending whether it is necessary
to keep the bush more upright or more open. Summer
prune the side growths in June about half-way back. It
is these growths that are pruned back harder still in the
winter. Keep the varieties with a drooping habit upright
by always cutting the leaders to an upright bud.

QUANTITY METHOD

Aim at developing seven or eight branches during the
first two or three years by the normal cutting back of the
leaders by about half but after that just cut out sufficient
old wood to keep the bush open, and allow for easy
picking. No cutting back will be done other than
removing the crossing branches, cutting out the dead
wood, and taking out a branch here and there to let in
the light and air. Branches should never be allowed to
trail on the ground as it is from the soil that the spores of
Mildew come.

MANURING HINTS

Gooseberries like both potash and nitrogen but there
is no doubt that potash is the more important of the two.
If you don't give gooseberry bushes potash regularly the
leaves show brown edges and this scorch prevents the
bushes from cropping heavily. Every year, therefore,
give sulphate of potash at $1\frac{1}{2}$ ounces to the square yard
or finely divided wood ashes at $\frac{1}{2}$ lb. per square yard.

Nitrogen is best applied in an organic form. Pig manure, poultry manure, and meat and bone meal are all useful, and in addition to giving the nitrogen they help to hold the moisture in the soil which is a valuable adjunct during a dry season. The poultry manure, however, should always be strawy or peaty. It is not wise to give dried concentrated poultry manure. Apply the pig dung at half bucketful per bush; the strawy poultry manure at the same rate and the meat and bone meal at 4 ounces per square yard. Properly composted vegetable refuse is also useful if used at a bucketful per square yard.

ROUTINE WORK

The great thing with gooseberries is to give them plenty of room for development. They won't do their best if they are crowded together. In addition, see that the branches are not allowed to trail on the ground. This always encourages Mildew and keep the bushes open so that it is easy to pick the fruits.

NOVEMBER
Do all the pruning necessary.

DECEMBER
Spray the bushes with a good tar distillate wash or with D.N.C. Apply sulphate of potash at 1½ ounces per square yard or use wood ashes at ½ lb. per square yard.

JANUARY
Apply organic manure and fork in very lightly.

MAY
Give the remainder of the organic manure as a top dressing or a mulch.

JUNE
Be ready to spray with Liquid Derris to control caterpillar and be ready to spray with lime-sulphur to prevent American Gooseberry Mildew.
Start picking the earliest berries.

JULY
Start picking the dessert varieties as they ripen.

NOTES ON ROUTINE WORK

(a) **Pruning.** Some people delay their pruning until the Spring so as to be able to see which buds the birds have left. It is better, however, to black cotton the bushes thoroughly after pruning in November and so prevent the birds from eating the buds.

(b) **Picking.** It is possible to pick the green berries as soon as they are ⅜ inch in diameter. Keep on picking, thinning the berries out as you do so. The berries you leave behind will keep on growing. Leave some berries on to gather when ripe.

VARIETIES

LIST OF BEST VARIETIES FOR SMALL GARDEN

GREEN	RED
Howard's Lancer (M.S.).	Whinham's Industry (M.S.)
Keepsake (E).	Lord Derby (L).

YELLOW	WHITE
Leveller (M.S.).	Careless (M.S.).
Leader (L).	Whitesmith (M.S.)

M.S. — Mid Season.   E — Early.   L — Late.

BEST VARIETIES FOR BOTTLING AND CANNING

Howard's Lancer.	Careless.
Keepsake.	Whinham's Industry.

BEST VARIETIES FOR VERY EARLY PICKING
GREEN

Careless.	Keepsake
Lancashire Lad.	White Lion.

BEST VERY LARGE FRUITS, WHEN RIPE

GREEN	RED	YELLOW	WHITE
Green Ocean.	London.	Broom Girl.	Careless.
Stockwell.	Lord Derby.	Leveller.	White Lion.

BEST VARIETIES FOR CORDONS

GREEN	RED	YELLOW	WHITE
Langley Gage.	Ironmonger.	Broom Girl.	Careless.
	Red Champagne.	Leveller.	Whitesmith.
	May Duke.	Keepsake.	

E

PESTS AND DISEASES. *Practical Points.*

Caterpillars. These fall into two groups—the Winter Moth Group that will damage the leaves and blossom and young berries and the Sawfly Group whose caterpillars gobble up all the leaves and can defoliate a whole bush in a day or two. Answer: In the case of the Winter Moth caterpillars it is important to smother all the eggs by spraying with a good tar distillate wash in December. In the case of the Sawfly Group spray with Liquid Derris immediately they are seen.

Green Fly (aphids). Green Flies suck the sap and cause the young shoots to become stunted and malformed. They will be found in large colonies in May and June. Answer: Spray with tar distillate wash in December and kill the eggs.

Red Spider. These will attack the foliage and it will turn grey or silvery as a result of the sucking of the sap by the spiders. In severe attacks the young leaves will be stunted. Later many of the leaves may fall off and in bad attacks the fruits will drop off. Answer: Spray with Di-nitro-ortho-cresol in December to kill hibernating mites and with lime-sulphur after blossoms have set with 1 pint to 60 pints water.

Mildew. Commonly found on the tips of the young shoots as a greyish-white thin felt. This can easily be rubbed off. Infection spreads to leaves when greyish-white blotches appear. These blotches spread to the berries which become covered with the greyish-white felt which turns brown. Answer: Spray with lime-sulphur at ½ pint to 10 gallons of water just before flowering and again with ¼ pint to 10 gallons water immediately after flowering. The·yellow varieties should not be sprayed with lime-sulphur but should be given a soda-soap solution instead, formula 2 lbs. washing soda, 1 lb. soap to 10 gallons water.

Die-Back. An affected branch suddenly wilts and dies. Whole bushes may be attacked in the same way. After death the bark peels off in flakes and greyish tufts will appear in damp weather in damp parts. Answer: Burn all affected wood immediately seen. Take care never to injure branches for any cracks or wounds will let in the fungus.

CHAPTER XI

DESSERT AND COOKING PEARS

THERE is no doubt that the pear is indigenous to Great Britain. It may still be found growing wild in some parts of the country, though in its wild state the fruits are of little value. It is undoubtedly one of the most delicious fruits to grow in the garden, but one of the most ticklish to tackle. Great care and attention have to be paid to pears if the best results are to be achieved. Garden conditions and climate can have a remarkable effect on the fruit. Pears always seem to do well in the vicinity of running water. The belt of pears along the Medway in Kent is typical of this.

SOIL AND SITUATION

Pears do not like badly drained clay soils nor do they care for light soils that dry out quickly or shallow soils over chalk or gravel. They will grow on most good garden soils with the exception of the later varieties which usually only do well in the South of England. The soil which is supposed to be the ideal is the brick earth of a medium type and one which is not only deep but well drained.

Late keeping pears have to be grown under the most perfect conditions and these include sunny sheltered places and a dry ripening season in the autumn. For this reason in the North most of the late varieties of pears are grown in cool greenhouses. Some of the simpler pears like Conference, Williams and Laxton's Superb do quite well even in the North of England, while the commoner pears like Hessle and Fertility will do well almost anywhere.

Never try and plant pears on a north wall with the

69

exception, perhaps, of a cooking variety like Uvedale St. Germain. All pear trees against walls will need protection from frost in the spring and ordinary fish netting will do this work well.

TREES TO BUY

As pears need more sunshine on the whole than apples and as on the whole they are slower in coming into bearing it is quite a good plan to purchase pear trees as cordons, as fuseaux, and as pyramids. Bush trees do quite well, especially if the branches are well spaced, and spur pruning is carried out. Cordons however are easy to look after and as more cordons can be planted than any other type, owing to the little room they take up, those with small gardens will probably prefer them.

ROOT STOCKS

It is most important to buy trees guaranteed grafted on the right stocks and then having purchased them to see that the trees are planted shallowly. When trees are planted deeply there is always the danger that the variety of pear will send out roots and so mask or ruin the effect the stock should have. Take for example a Williams grafted on a Quince A stock. If you plant the tree deeply, then roots will grow out from the Williams wood and ruin the effect of the Quince roots which should be controlling the life of the tree. No pear tree, therefore should be planted deeper than, say, 8 inches.

Probably the best stock for the cordons is the Quince C. This is very dwarfing in its effect and trees grafted on it come into cropping quickly. The Quince A is the best stock for the bush, fuseau, or pyramid type of tree, or even for espaliers.

Unfortunately some varieties of pears are incompatible when grafted on to Quince stocks. In these cases it is necessary to graft the trees first of all with another variety and then to graft this variety with the incompatible one. This, of course, is the problem of the nurseryman rather than the purchaser, but the information is given here so that the gardener may know that some of the pear trees have to be double-worked as it is called, and the nurseryman may expect to be paid a little more for a tree which has to be raised in this way.

The younger the trees are when planted the better. Always put in two year olds or one year olds. Bush and pyramid trees need to be 12 ft. square, while fuseau can be 6 ft. by 3ft. Single cordons should be planted 2 ft. apart and be trained at an angle of 45 degrees against the wires.

PRUNING HINTS

As a general rule the side shoots or lateral growths should be cut back to within two or three buds of their base, and this will help to produce fruit buds. The leaders or end growths will be cut back by about half to just above an outward pointing bud, or in the case of branches that are tending to spread, to just above an inward pointing bud.

During the first three or four years it may be necessary to cut the leaders somewhat harder in order to produce strong branches and the side growths could be left alone. It must be remembered that the general rule is, the less winter pruning a young tree receives, the sooner it will come into bearing. Once, however, a tree has started to crop heavily, it is usually necessary to prune the leaders fairly hard so as to ensure that the tree grows well.

When pear trees are old they often become covered with fruit buds and in this case it is usually necessary to thin these out. In bad cases every other spur can be cut out completely. Where such drastic treatment is not thought necessary, the spur could be shortened back so as to remove a number of the fruit buds. A tree will only

set a certain amount of blossom satisfactorily and it is
foolish to allow a tree to produce very many more flowers
than are required.

In the summer it is a good plan to cut back the side
growths or laterals to within 2 inches or so of their base
as soon as the growths get woody, that is when they are
about 8 inches long. This usually means starting summer
pruning early in June and continuing once a month until
September. Those who do not wish this continuous form
of summer pruning should just cut back all the side
growth to about the fifth leaf in July.

Some varieties of pears are tip bearers, e.g., Jargonelle
and in this case to prune back the laterals is, of course, a
mistake. Gardeners should watch the habits of the tree
when pruning and work accordingly.

MANURIAL HINTS

Every winter dig in shallowly around the trees farmyard manure or well-rotted composted vegetable refuse
at the rate of half a bucketful to the square yard. In
January give sulphate of potash at 1 ounce to the square
yard and if the trees set a heavy crop in the Spring,
give in addition sulphate of ammonia at $\frac{1}{2}$ ounce to the
square yard, plus superphosphate at 2 ounces to the
square yard. Where composted vegetable refuse or
farmyard manure are not obtainable, hop manure or
wool shoddy manure may be used instead.

POLLINATION HINTS

Do not forget that a large number of pears are self-
sterile. They will not produce friut with their own
pollen. See, therefore, that varieties are planted nearby
which will produce the right blossom at the right time.
Under the heading of Varieties, self-fertile varieties will
be found, and all the rest may be said to be self-sterile.
There is much to be said for only planting self-fertile
varieties in the small garden.

ROUTINE WORK

Much of the routine work is concerned with watering and mulching. Wall trees, for instance, often suffer from lack of water in a dry summer time. A good mulching with lawn mowings or similar material in the early summer will do much to keep a heavy crop of pears going.

NOVEMBER
Get all the pruning done and the prunings burnt.

DECEMBER
Spray the trees with a good tar distillate wash.

JANUARY
Apply the farmyard manure, compost vegetable refuse, and dig in shallowly. Apply the sulphate of potash.

APRIL
Get ready to spray the trees just before the blossom opens, with lime-sulphur to keep down Scab. If a heavy crop sets give the sulphate of ammonia and superphosphate.

MAY
Spray again with lime-sulphur directly after all the blossoms have fallen, as the second Scab Spray.
Start carrying out the continuous summer pruning method.

JUNE
Apply a mulching of decaying organic matter around the trees, especially those growing against walls. In very dry weather a good flooding with water may be necessary.
Thin out the pears if a heavy crop has set. Leave no fruit closer than 6 inches apart.

JULY
Carry out the ordinary summer pruning if the continuous method has not been adopted. Put bags on fruits to keep away wasps.

AUGUST-SEPTEMBER
Picking early varieties.

OCTOBER
Continue picking.

SPECIAL HINTS ON ROUTINE WORK

(a) Thinning. Tend to thin the varieties which usually carry small fruits more drastically than those which bear large fruits. A variety like Fertility, for instance, generally needs severe thinning while a variety like Pitmaston Duchess which produces a large pear, seldom needs thinning.

(b) **Wasp Protectors.** Paper bags, butter muslin bags, or net bags can all be used popped over the fruits and tied to the spurs to prevent birds and wasps from damaging the fruits as they are ripening. They also stop the fruits from dropping to the ground.

(c) **Picking.** Gather the early and mid-season varieties when the stock comes easily away from the spur. Some varieties like Williams should be picked before they are yellow for they go soft so quickly. Later varieties can be stored as advised for apples. If possible always keep pears in separate store from apples for one seems to affect the other. Wrap pears in plain paper not in oiled paper wraps. Pears keep best when stored at a temperature of between 40-45 degrees F. where there is plenty of air, plus darkness. Do not store in too dry a place or the fruit will shrivel.

VARIETIES

SELF-FERTILES

EARLY FLOWERERS	MID-SEASON FLOWERERS	LATE FLOWERERS
Conference	Fertility	Hessle
Durrondeau	Marie Louise	Dr. Jules Guyot
Jargonelle	Williams	Pitmaston Duchess
Margaret Marillat	Buerré Bedford	
Bergamotte	Bellissime d'Hiver	
D'Esperen	Laxton's Superb	

AUGUST-SEPTEMBER PEARS

Williams	Dr. Jules Guyot	Jargonelle
Hessle	Laxton's Superb	Souvenir de Congres

OCTOBER-NOVEMBER PEARS

Conference	Doyenne du Comice	Durrondeau
Margaret Marillat	Marie Louise	Pitmaston Duchess

NOVEMBER-DECEMBER PEARS

Glou Morceau	Josephine de Malines	Winter Nelis
Passe Colmar	Beurré Easter	Beurré Rance

THREE BEST PEARS FOR SMALL GARDEN

Conference	Laxton's Superb	Dr. Jules Guyot

COOKING PEARS

Catillac	Uvedale St. Germain	Vicar of Wakefield

BEST FLAVOURED PEARS

Williams, Sept.	Marie Louise, Oct.	Doyenne du Comice, Nov.
Winter Nelis, Dec.	Thompson's, Oct.-Nov.	Comte de Lamy, Oct.-Nov.

PESTS AND DISEASES. *Practical Points.*

Maggots in Pears. May be caused by either the Codlin Moth, and in this case the larvæ enter the eye and ruin the fruit as in apples, or the Pear Midge, which gets into the fruits as soon as they have set and cause them to swell abnormally. Their centres will be found to consist of black rotten material together with numerous white legless maggots. Answer: In the case of the Codlin Moth, spray with arsenate of lead late in June or early in July. In the case of the Pear Midge, run poultry under the trees in April, May and June; hoe the ground regularly in June and July and pick off all infected fruit immediately it is seen.

Slug Worm. A little pest which looks like a slug, found on the upper surface of the leaves, eating away the tissue. Answer: Dust the trees thoroughly with Derris Dust.

Blister Mite. Blisters or pimples will be found on the young leaves in the spring. Usually red in colour. Sometimes the fruits will be attacked. Answer: Spray with lime-sulphur immediately the leaves have fallen to kill the insect which spends the winter under the bud scales.

Scab. Similar to the Apple Scab, which please see on page 47. Causes black spots on leaves and fruits and in bad cases will cause fruits to crack and be ruined. Young pear wood can also be affected and produce scabby wood. Answer: Spray with lime-sulphur just before the blossoms open, 1 pint to 30 pints water. Spray again with this brown liquid, 1 pint to 60 pints water, immediately all the blossoms have fallen.

Chapter XII

DESSERT AND COOKING PLUMS

PLUMS are always useful to have in the garden, for not only are they excellent for dessert but they make good jam and can be dried and made into prunes. Many of the types of wild plums like the bullace, are indigenous to the country and even to-day are found growing wild in hedges and copses. The cultivated plums of to-day were introduced in the 16th Century from Europe while latterly some varieties have come to us from America. Nurserymen in this country have not been slow to introduce new varieties and Laxton's of Bedford have done much to this end.

SOIL AND SITUATION

Plums love rich garden soil. They dislike the heavy clays, the light sands or very chalky ground but they will put up with chalk if there is a good loam above. They are liable to frost damage and should always be grown where they can be sheltered from North and East winds at blossoming time. They do better on high land than on low land. When plum trees are grown against walls they should always be sheltered at blossoming time with fish netting.

TREES TO BUY

Unfortunately there is no good dwarfing stock as there is in the case of pears and so it is difficult to grow a plum tree successfully as a bush. For this reason plums are usually grown as half-standards in a garden, though it is quite possible to have bush trees if they are not pruned hard. Fan-trained trees on a wall are excellent providing that plenty of room can be given. It is not advisable to plant plums as cordons.

ROOT STOCKS

Myrobolan B is perhaps the best stock where strong growth is required coupled with regular cropping.

The Common Plum stock is dwarfing and is recommended for the variety Victoria. It is not, however, very suitable for other varieties.

PRUNING HINTS

It is better to prune plums as little as possible. In fact some of the best plum growers leave their plum trees absolutely unpruned after the first two years except for cutting out crossing branches, rubbing wood and dead or diseased wood.

For the first two or three years it is a good plan to form good branches by cutting back the leaders or end growths by half to just above a bud. The laterals or side growths need not be pruned.

With wall trees some of the old wood should be cut out each year and the new wood should be tied in, in its place. Any side growths not required for tying in should be pinched back to six leaves in the summer. The tying in to position of the replacement shoots should be done in September.

Because plum trees are very liable to Silver Leaf, a disease which spreads very quickly, some gardeners prefer to do all the pruning required in the summer. Silver Leaf spores are not about then or if they are, they cannot enter an open wound because of the rising sap. Therefore where this disease abounds, carry out all pruning during the months of June, July and August.

Trees that are growing against fences or walls, generally have to be root pruned or they grow too strongly. Three years after planting they should be dug up and about half the roots should be cut away. A similar pruning may be done every four or five years after that.

MANURING HINTS

Plums like plenty of nitrogen. Every year give heavy dressings of well rooted organic matter, applying farmyard manure or composted vegetable refuse at the rate of one bucketful to the square yard. This should be dug in during the winter cultivations. The ground beneath plum trees should always be well hoed and kept free from weeds. In February sulphate of ammonia or nitro chalk should be applied at 1 oz to the square yard and hoed in lightly, whilst on very sandy soils, sulphate of potash may be necessary in addition at 1 oz. to the square yard. This should be applied in December.

ROUTINE WORK

It is possible to concentrate most of the work on plums in the summer. For instance, the pruning can be done then, the mulching with organic matter to keep in the moisture, the thinning of the fruits and so on.

NOVEMBER
Do what pruning is necessary if this has not been done in the summer.
DECEMBER
Spray with a good tar distillate wash, using a 5 per cent. solution. Apply sulphate of potash if necessary.
FEBRUARY
Apply sulphate of ammonia or nitro chalk and dig in organic matter lightly if not already dug in in December or January.
JUNE
Thin fruits, especially on trees with heavy crops.
AUGUST-SEPTEMBER
Pick fruits.
OCTOBER
Spray trees with Bordeaux mixture to prevent Bacterial Canker.

NOTES ON ROUTINE WORK:
(a) Picking. In the case of dessert varieties, leave individual fruits on trees until thoroughly ripe. Never pick when wet. Pick cooking plums directly they turn colour.
(b) Thinning. Thin fruits to 2½ ins. apart. Never allow any plums closer than this. Support laden branches with wires or posts to prevent them breaking.

VARIETIES

With plums there are the same difficulties with regard to pollination as with pears. See page 72. In a small garden, therefore, only palnt self-fertile varieties or if self-sterile kinds must be planted, see that the correct mate or husband is planted at the same time nearby.

THE BEST SELF FERTILE VARIETIES

EARLY FLOWERERS	MID-SEASON FLOWERERS	LATE FLOWERERS
Early Laxton's	Czar	Oullin's Golden Gage
Early Transparent Gage	Victoria	Blaisdon Red
Monarch	Purple Egg	Belle de Louvain
Denniston's Superb Gage	Laxton's Gage	
	Paxton's Prosperity	
	Evesham Wonder	

GARDEN PLUMS FOR SUCCESSION

Dennison's Superb, August	Oullin's Golden Gage, Mid-August
Laxton's Gage, late August	Victoria, early September
Bryanston Gage, Mid-September	Kirk's Blue, Mid-September
Coe's Golden Drop, late September	Golden Transparent Gage, Early October

PLUMS FOR WALLS OR FENCES

SOUTH	EAST	WEST
Kirk's Blue	Coe's Golden Drop	Victoria
Coe's Golden Drop	Victoria	Kirke's Blue
Jefferson's Gage	Kirke's Blue	Bryanston Gage
Early Transparent Gage	Angelina Burdett	Jefferson's Gage

NORTH		
Belle de Louvain		
Dennison's Superb Gage		
Victoria		
Oullin's Golden Gage		

BEST PLUMS FOR FANS

Cambridge Gage	Dennison's Superb		Laxton's Gage
Washington	Early Orleans		Comte d'Althan's Gage
Bryanston Gage			
Monarch			

BEST PLUMS FOR BUSHES

Victoria	Czar	River's Early	Purple Pershore
Giant Prune	Belle de Louvain	Transparent Gage	Early Orleans

PESTS AND DISEASES. *Practical Points.*

(a) *Green Fly* (Aphides). There are three types of aphides which attack plums. There is the leaf-curling type which attacks the shoots and stunts them. It may cause the fruit to remain small, and in this case it will drop to the ground, and of course it curls the leaves. The Mealy type which doesn't curl the leaves but becomes abundant in mid-summer, producing quantities of sticky secretion which may spoil the fruits and ruin the leaves. The Hop aphis which attacks damsons more than plums, feeding on the leaves till May or early June. Answer: The answer in all three cases is to spray the trees thoroughly with a good tar distillate wash in December.

(b) *Red Spider.* The leaves go yellowy-brown in colour and if the underneath surface is examined a white thread-like substance appears, and if looked at with a magnifying glass tiny little yellow egg-like insects will be seen. Answer: Spray with lime-sulphur at 1 pint to 100 pints water ten days after petal fall. Spray in December with Di-nitro-ortho-cresol.

(c) *Maggots.* May be caused by the Sawfly or the Red Plum Maggot. In the case of the Sawfly, the eggs are laid in the flowers at blossoming time. The maggots attack the fruits which usually drop off when small and green. In the case of the Red Plum Maggot the eggs are laid on the fruits early in July and the minute caterpillars tunnel into the fruit, usually unseen, but a red maggot will be found with a lot of frass when the fruit is eaten. Answer: Spray with plenty of Liquid Derris early in July.

(d) *Bacterial Canker.* The leaves on a branch will turn yellow, wither any time from May to August. Sometimes a trunk is attacked and then the whole tree looks sick. Infection is usually accompanied by the oozing of gum. Often the leaves have a shot hole effect. Tiny little holes appear all over them. Answer: Spray the trunks of the trees thoroughly with Bordeaux Mixture just before the leaves fall.

(e) *Brown Rot.* The fruit goes brown and rots on the tree. It will be found to have rings of buff coloured fungus on it. Sometimes the tips of the shoots die and the spur on which the fruit is borne is killed. Other times the flowers are killed by the fungus. Answer: Spray with a good tar distillate wash in December, 1 pint to 10 pints of water. Spray with lime-sulphur, 1 pint to 50 pints water just before flowering and give a thorough soaking.

(f) *Silver Leaf.* The leaves have a silver sheen on them any time during the summer. This is due to air pockets in the leaf and not to a fungus layer outside. The centre of the wood of the branch will be affected and here a brown stain will be found. Later the wood will die, and bracket fungi will appear. Answer: All dead wood must be cut out and burnt before the 15th July each year by a Government Order. The wounds must be painted with thick white lead paint. Rust. Orange yellow spots will be found on the leaves, usually on the underside. Later the spots turn dark brown. Answer: Spray early in June with Bordeaux Mixture, giving a thorough covering. In bad cases spray again three weeks later with colloidal copper.

CHAPTER XIII

CANE FRUITS

RASBERRIES, LOGANBERRIES, BLACKBERRIES, ETC.
THERE are a large number of cane fruits grown in this country. The most important are undoubtedly the raspberry, loganberry and blackberry. Other canes like the Low Berry, the Boysenberry, the Veitch Berry are grown in a similar manner to the loganberry and those who are wanting to try these unusual types of cane fruits will be able to do so on the lines laid down for loganberries. The Young berry is said to be an intermediate between the Low Berry and the Dew Berry. The Phenomenal Berry is very similar to the New Berry. The King's Acre Berry is very much like a large blackberry. There are numbers of them and it is not proposed to describe them in this book. They are not sufficiently important.

THE RASPBERRY

This is indigenous to Great Britain. It can be found again and again up and down the country, growing wild in the copses and hedges. In its wild form it produces a poor type of fruit, mostly pips. As the result of the plant breeder's work there are many delicious types of raspberries on offer to-day. One of the leading raspberry raisers is undoubtedly Mr. Pyne, of Topsham, Devon.

SOIL AND SITUATION

Most garden soils will do raspberries well. They will put up with fairly bad drainage as a rule and they are certainly very hardy. They prefer a rich deep, well-drained soil, and always do best under such conditions. They are particularly keen on plenty of organic matter.

CANES TO BUY

Always buy one year old canes from a stock which is guaranteed to be virus free. It is a great mistake to purchase canes from any unknown source. Each year young canes are thrown up from the roots and it is these that bear the following season. Directly new canes have been planted they should be cut down to within 6 inches of ground level. It is a mistake to allow newly-planted canes to crop the following year.

HOW TO PROPAGATE

Suckers, as they may be called, grow up alongside the raspberry rows and these canes, more usually called spawn, are severed from their parent plants in November and are planted out into a new row. It is most important however, only to save canes from plants that are known to be free from virus disease, and therefore, a keen raspberry grower will take pains to learn how to distinguish virus. He should study the Notes given at the end of the chapter, and may go to inspect virus infected plants at his County Horticultural Centre where demonstrational work of this kind may be going on.

PLANTING HINTS

Try and get the canes planted in November or early December. Set them in rows 6 ft. apart with the canes 2 ft. apart in the rows. Plant shallowly. The top roots should never be in deeper than 1 inch below the surface of the ground. On the other hand, plant firmly. Cut the newly-planted canes down to within 6 inches of soil level the following March.

PRUNING HINTS

Each autumn cut the old canes—that is those that have borne the fruit, down to ground level; at the same time cut down to ground level the weakest shoots in each clump, leaving six strong canes in the case of each clump.

In March cut back the canes 1 ft. so as to encourage
the breaking out of side growths on which more fruit
will be borne. In June go over the cane rows and if any
suckers are coming up in between the rows cut these out
with a sharp spade right away.

There are autumn fruiting types of raspberries which
bear their berries in September and October, and some
even in November if the weather is mild. In this case
the canes should be cut down to within 4 inches of soil
level in February. Th new crop of canes develops in the
summer, and it is these that crop in the autumn.

GROWING HINTS

Raspberry canes will usually need some support; if
wires are stretched tightly between posts at either ends of

the rows, say 3 ft. and 5 ft. from the ground level, the
canes can be tied to these.

A simpler method is to have a post at either end of the
row and nail to this a T piece 18 inches to 2 ft. long,
and to strain from either end of the T piece, strong wire.
The canes are then allowed to grow in between the

parallel wires thus formed and no tying is necessary Double T pieces, one at 5 ft. and the other at 3 ft. are sometimes used. (See drawing.)

A good deal of water may have to be given when the fruit is swelling, if the weather is dry. Mulchings with well-rotted vegetable refuse should also be made along the rows, early in June. Regular hoeing along the rows is also advisable and necessary.

MANURING HINTS

In May or early June apply lawn mowings, well-rotted dung or composted vegetable refuse along the rows. This can be forked in lightly in the autumn. All cultivations must be shallow because the roots are near the surface.

In addition apply sulphate of potash at 1½ ounces per square yard each February, and give Cornish Fish Manure at 3 ounces to the yard run at the same time. Hoe these in lightly.

ROUTINE WORK. The routine work is really very simple.

OCTOBER
Carry out the normal pruning.

DECEMBER
Spray the canes with a tar distillate wash, using a 5 per cent. solution.

FEBRUARY
Cut canes of autumn fruiting varieties to within 4 ins. ground level.

MARCH
Cut back tops of canes to encourage side growths.

MAY-JUNE
Put mulchings of dung or well-rotted vegetable refuse along rows.

JUNE
Remove all suckers in between rows.

JULY-AUGUST
Pick fruit.

SPECIAL HINTS ON ROUTINE WORK.

(a) *Picking.* Fruit for jam is usually picked straight off the cane without the plug. Fruit for dessert is often picked with the plug. For jam it is a good plan to leave the berries on the canes as long as possible.

VARIETIES

SUMMER FRUITING

VARIETY	SEASON	REMARKS
Lloyd George	July	Heavy cropper. Young canes often give berries in the autumn as well.
Norfolk Giant	Late	Large round berries, heavy cropper.
Pyne's Royal	Summer	Lovely dessert fruit.
Baumforth Seedling A.	Summer	Best for jam.
Preussen	Summer	Sweet, good flavour, rather soft.

AUTUMN FRUITING

VARIETY	SEASON	REMARKS
Hailsham Berry	Oct.-Nov.	Large fruit. Vigorous grower.
November Abundance	November	Large fruit. Well flavoured.
October Red	October	Large fruit. Very prolific.

YELLOW VARIETIES

VARIETY	SEASON	REMARKS
Superlative	Summer	Large fruit.
Antwerp	Summer	Very pleasant flavour. Sweet.
Golden Hornet	Summer	Large, good flavour.

PESTS AND DISEASES. *Practical Points.*

Beetle. A small brownish beetle; lays eggs in the flowers. These hatch out into dirty white maggots which ruin the fruits. Answer: Spray with liquid derris at the end of June. Soak the canes thoroughly.

Moth. The moths lay their eggs in the blossoms. Caterpillars hatch out which feed inside the berries but are not seen. When half grown they change to a red colour and drop to the ground where they spin a coccoon. In April they climb up the canes and feed on the lateral shoots which are growing, ruining them. Answer: Look for attacked shoots and destroy caterpillars. If serious, spray with liquid derris.

The spraying in December with tar distillate wash will do good, especially if soil on either side of the canes is given a good soaking.

Virus. The leaves are mottled with yellow. They are often curled downwards. The canes fail to grow strongly and cease to crop heavily. Very susceptible varieties are Baumforth's Seedling B, Superlative and Lloyd George. Answer: Dig up infected canes and burn them.

Cane Spot. Purplish spots appear on the canes early in Summer. These will get larger and the centres will become greyer. Spots may run together and cause cankers. Answer: Spray just as the buds start to grow in the Spring with a 7 per cent. solution of lime-sulphur. Give a thorough soaking.

Blue Stripe Wilt. A broad bluey brown stripe will be found towards the base of the cane. The older leaves of young canes usually show a dark brown colour between the main veins. Answer: Correct manuring helps as does regular hoeing. Affected canes usually recover naturally.

LOGANBERRIES

The Loganberry is said to be a cross between the raspberry and the blackberry. It is certainly very similar to the Phenomenal Berry though the latter ripens somewhat later. It is a very vigorous grower, much more like the blackberry than the raspberry and the fruit it produces is more suited to cooking and bottling than to be eaten as dessert. The berry never separates from the centre plug when picked. The loganberry may be trained against wire netting, against fences and against wire screens erected especially for the purpose.

SOIL AND SITUATION

Choose a spot where there are no draughts. Protection from excessive winds is necessary. Will grow in almost any soil but prefers a deep loam which is well drained. Likes plenty of organic matter. Revels in rich land.

CANES TO BUY

Purchase what are known as Tips, in February or early March. The writer has had better results with planting at this time than in the autumn. The tips should be purchased from well-known nurserymen for there has been much confusion in the past and poor types of logan-berries have been sold.

How to Propagate

Propagation is done by the method known as Tip Rooting. The tip of a young growth in the June is buried in the soil 2 or 3 inches down. The result is that roots develop and a shoot grows upwards and this rooted tip can then be severed the following April. Rooting is best done in June or early July, though tip propagation has been carried out as late as the second week of August. Some gardeners prefer to sink into the ground a 1 lb. chip basket full of a soil compost consisting of three parts soil, three parts peat, and one part sand. The tip is then buried in this and rooting takes place readily. Next February the basket is dug up which will by now be filled with roots. The plant, basket and all, can then be set out in its new position and this gives the least root disturbance. Chip baskets soon rot away and the plants grow well.

Pruning Hints

The canes which have borne a crop are cut down to the ground in the autumn and the young canes that have grown during the summer are then tied up in their place. In order to prevent the disease spores from the old canes dropping down on to the young canes it is a good plan to train the old canes on wires say, stretched up to 5 ft., and to tie the new canes as they grow, up in between the centre of the old canes and on to a wire stretched above them.

Another method is to train the young canes to form the left part of the fan, the old canes then being the right part of the fan. The following year the old canes are cut away and the new canes are then tied up in their place, so you get new and old canes alternately on the left and right hand side of this fan training method. (See drawing.)

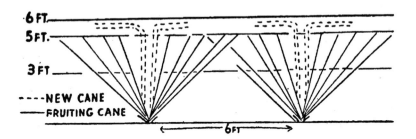

MANURING HINTS

Every year a good dressing of farmyard manure or properly composted vegetable refuse should be forked or dug in lightly in the late autumn at the rate of one good bucketful to the square yard. In addition, in March, Cornish Fish Manure should be applied at 2 ounces to the square yard and sulphate of potash at 1 ounce to the square yard. Some gardeners like to give steamed bone flour in addition at 2 ounces to the square yard.

ROUTINE WORK

NOVEMBER
Cut the old canes down the ground level and tie the new canes firmly up into position. Fork in well-rotted vegetable refuse at one bucket full to the square yard.

DECEMBER
Spray the canes with a good tar distillate wash using a 5 per cent. solution.

MARCH
Apply Cornish Fish Manure, sulphate of potash and steamed bone flour.

MAY
Hoe regularly along rows.

JUNE
Strike tips. Give mulchings of lawn mowings or well-rotted vegetable refuse along rows.
AUGUST-SEPTEMBER
Pick fruit.

Special Hints on Routine Work

In some areas loganberries will ripen as early as the middle of July and in some areas they will keep on till the middle of September. Always pick when the berries are dry.

Diseases and Pests. Practical Points.

Beetle. This is the same trouble that attacks the raspberry. Please note remarks made under this heading.

Moth. See raspberry.

Cane Spot. For recognition see raspberry. Answer: Spray just before the blossoms open with Bordeaux Mixture and again just before the fruits ripen, with colloidal copper.

BLACKBERRY

No one will doubt the Author when he states that the blackberry is indigenous to this country and will be found in hedgerows in North, South, East and West. It is said that the cultivated blackberry has not such a fine flavour as its wild brother, but there are certainly great advantages in picking large, well-ripened berries in one's own garden, rather than picking smaller berries from the hedges which may or may not be there!

Soil and Situation

The blackberry will grow almost anywhere in the garden. It doesn't seem to be particular as to soil. Undoubtedly it likes a sunny situation and land that is well drained. Like the loganberry it revels in plenty of organic matter.

Canes to Buy

Blackberry tips should be purchased, very much in the same way as advised for loganberries. Be sure to go to a reliable nurseryman who can guarantee the correct name. Remember that the blackberry takes up a lot of room. It will need, say, 16 ft. of wire if it is going to grow and crop its heaviest.

How to Propagate.—See loganberries.

Pruning Hints

Blackberries grow very strongly and have prickly canes. The pruning is better done, therefore, wearing gloves. As to the method of pruning and training, please see loganberries. Remember on the whole the blackberries grow even stronger than the loganberries.

Manuring Hints

Generous manuring is necessary. Every late autumn dig in farmyard manure or composted vegetable refuse at one pailful per square yard. In addition in March apply Cornish Fish manure at 3 ounces to the square yard, sulphate of potash at 1 ounce per square yard and steamed bone flour at 2 ounces to the square yard.

Routine Work.—See loganberries.

Varieties

Name	Description	Remarks
Himalaya	Strong grower, large black berries. Heavy cropper.	Very similar to Black Diamond.
John Innes	Very late in ripening. Heavy cropper.	Raised by Mr. M. B. Crane.
Parsley-Leaved	Decorative, large black fruit. Heavy cropper.	Self-fertile.
Bedfordshire Giant	Ripens in July. Very large berries. Good quality.	Raised by Messrs. Laxtons.

Chapter XIV

STRAWBERRIES

THE strawberry is indigenous to Great Britain and is often found growing on the Downs, in woods and even in grass land. Most of the cultivated strawberries to-day came originally from Chile and Virginia. There have been many breeders like Messrs. Laxtons, of Bedford, who specialise in producing new varieties.

There are also the Alpine strawberries and what are called the Perpetual Fruiting strawberries which have arisen as a result of the cross between the normal large fruiting kinds and the Alpines.

SOIL AND SITUATION

The strawberry prefers land that is rich in humus. It has always been said to prefer land that has recently been a wood copse, because of the residues of leaves that are left behind. Some varieties like Royal Sovereign like the lighter soils, while others like Huxley's Giant, prefer the heavier types. The great thing is to have plenty of finely divided organic matter in top 4 or 5 inches. It is quite a good plan, therefore, before planting strawberries, to apply finely divided peat at 1 lb. per square yard, and fork this in lightly.

Choose a situation that is frost-free. Choose a sunny place so that the fruit can ripen well. Don't plant underneath apple trees or other fruits where the drips from the tar distillate wash may injure the plants in December.

PLANTS TO BUY

Be very careful from whom you buy your plants. Always purchase guaranteed virus-free stock. It is

93

always wise to purchase material that has come from the East Malling Research Station. Those who do not know where such strawberries may be obtained should contact the Author. One year old plants should be purchased and the new beds should always be made, if possible, in July or August. September planting is permissible but it is a great mistake to plant in October and November. Spring planting is to be preferred to late planting, but there is no doubt that July or August plantings are much the most successful.

How to Propagate

Young runners grow out from the one year old plants in June and early July. At distances along the stolons or runners, plants develop and these if pushed gently into the soil, or are held in place with a hair pin, root quickly. Only allow perfectly healthy plants to produce runners, and these runners usually take the place of their August and put them out into their permanent positions as soon as possible. It is always a good plan to set aside a few plants for runner production in a part of the garden separate from the plants that have been grown for fruiting. These parent plants should be sprayed regularly with nicotine and soap to keep them free from pests, particularly aphides which are said to be the carriers of the virus diseases which are so deadly to strawberries.

Alpine strawberries are propagated by seed sowing in the spring or in the autumn. Once the plants are raised they should be set out 1 ft. apart.

Perpetual fruiting strawberries are propagated by runners and these runners usually take the place of their parents which are scrapped at the end of one bearing season.

Planting Hints

Early planting, as has already been said, is very important. To ensure good early plants some gardeners

cause the runner plants to strike in 3 inch pots, plunged
in the ground to their rims, containing a good compost,
as advised for loganberries. See page 89. One runner
plant is pegged down in the centre of each pot.

The planting should be done in the prepared ground
in an open situation, 2½ ft. apart between the rows and
18 inches apart in the rows. The ground should be
absolutely clean and free from perennial weeds. It
should have been dug over well the previous winter and
farmyard manure and composted vegetable refuse should
be buried at the rate of one good barrowload to 12
square yards. In January the soil should receive
hydrated lime at 5-6 ounces to the square yard.

A crop of early vegetables can then be taken off a
patch of ground so as to leave the land free for the
strawberry planting in July or early August. All that
will be necessary then will be to fork the soil over lightly,
adding Cornish Fish manure at 3-4 ounces to the square
yard. Planting should always be done with a trowel so
that the roots of the strawberries may be spread out.
Firm planting is necessary and in such a manner that
the crown of the runner plant is just above the surface
of the soil.

A strawberry bed should last about three or four years.
It is usually impossible to keep the plants free from virus
longer than this, and so at the end of the third or fourth
fruiting season the strawberries are dug up and burned,
especially if there is any sign at all of disease.

CULTIVATION HINTS
It is important to hoe between the rows regularly and
shallowly, to keep down weeds and conserve the moisture.
When hoeing, the soil should be drawn towards the plants
rather than away from them.

POLLINATION HINTS
Some varieties of strawberries are self-sterile, that is
to say they need a husband; Tardive de Leopold, for

instance, needs Huxley; Oberschlesien will be pollinated by Huxley also. Oberschlesien, however, will not pollinate Huxley and Royal Sovereign has to be used for this purpose.

MANURING HINTS

Apply sulphate of potash in November at $1\frac{1}{2}$ ounces to the square yard and superphosphate at the same rate. Give Cornish Fish Manure early in May and hoe in.

ROUTINE WORK

JULY-AUGUST
Get the young strawberry plants put in as soon as possible.

NOVEMBER
Dig ground over for new strawberry beds. Bury the organic manure a spade's depth. Apply the sulphate of potash and superphosphate.

FEBRUARY
Go over ground and if any of the plants have been forced out by the frost, tread them in well.

APRIL
Give protection against frost if flowering, by covering with netting or with Continuous Cloches.

MAY
Hoe regularly.

JUNE
Put straw along the rows on which the flowers may be lying. This keeps the berries clean.
Protect aginst birds which eat the ripening fruits.

JULY
Propagate the runners from the one year old parent plants.

SPECIAL HINTS ON ROUTINE WORK

Picking. Don't pick strawberries when they are wet or they rot very quickly. Much earlier picking can be assured if the plants are grown under Continuous Cloches from April onwards.

VARIETIES

STRAWBERRIES

NAME	SEASON	REMARKS
Brenda Gautrey (sometimes called Huxley)	Mid-Season	Strong grower, good cropper, fruit large but coarse.
Oberschlesien	Mid-Season	Large fruit, heavy cropper, medium flavour.
Royal Sovereign	Early	Best flavoured variety grown.
Sir Joseph Paxton	Late	Good flavour, best for heavy soil.
Tardive de Leopold	Late	Large, good flavour, strong grower.
Waterloo	Late	Large, good flavour. Prefers light soil.

ALPINE STRAWBERRIES

VARIETIES	SEASON	REMARKS
Bush White	Summer & Autumn	Good flavour, produces no runners.
Gaillon Rouge	July-Oct.	Large fruits, crops well. No runners.
Alpine Improved	July-Oct.	Small, hardy prolific.

PERPETUAL FRUITING STRAWBERRIES

VARIETIES	SEASON	REMARKS
St. Anthony of Padua	Autumn	Prolific, large red fruits.
St. Joseph	July-Oct.	Medium fruits, good flavour.
St. Fiacre	July-Oct.	Hardy, bright red berries.

PESTS AND DISEASES. *Practical Points.*

Green Fly (Aphides). Pale green aphides, almost colourless, feed on leaves and stalks and suck sap. Usually a carrier of the virus diseases. Answer: Dip plants in nicotine and soft soap before planting. Spray with nicotine and soft soap in June and September.

Mites. Invisible except under a high powered glass. Live in folds of youngest leaves. Answer: Submerge young plants for twenty minutes in water which can be kept at 110 degrees F. exactly for this period. All young plants are best treated by this method. Cool plants down quickly afterwards by putting in cold water.

Beetles. Black shiney beetles eat the green and ripening berries. Answer: Sink jam jars into the soil and bait with small pieces of meat.

Weevil. Black beetle like insect. Lays its eggs in unopened flower buds at base. These wilt and shrivel. Answer: Dust with plenty of Derris Dust when blossom buds appears.

Mildew. Leaves and stems covered with a whitish mealy down. Berries in bad cases are attacked. Answer: Dust with sulphur dust immediately the trouble is seen. Dust again a week later.

Yellow Edge. A virus disease. The edges of the leaves go yellow. The plant is dwarfed and has a flattened appearance and the leaves go small and curved. Answer: Dig up and burn.

Crinkle. Crinkled leaves often appear with Yellow Edges as well. A virus. The young leaves go crinkly and often have brown spots on them. Answer: Dig up and burn.